Forth Rd Br

North Berwick

Dunbar

East Linton

Fast Castle

EDINBURGH

Tranent

Haddington

St Abb's Head

ngston

Dalkeith

Scottish East March

Eye Water

Eyemouth

Penicuik

Whiteadder Water

OTLAND

Duns

Berwick-upon-Tweed

Peebles

Lauder

Greenlaw

Blackadder Water

R Tweed

Norham Castle

Innerleithen

Galashiels

Melrose

Coldstream

Holy Island

Hume Castle

Etal Castle

Traquair

R Tweed

Smailholm Tower

Kelso

Flodden

Bamburgh Castle

MANOR HILLS

△ *Eildon Hills*

Ancrum Moor

R Glen

Homildon Hill

English East March

Seahouses

Dryhope Tower

Selkirk

Cessford Castle

The Cheviot

Wooler

aw △

St Mary's Loch

Ale Water

Jedburgh

Windy Gyle △

Alnwick

Resrs

Fatlips Castle

R Teviot

CHEVIOT HILLS

R Aln

at Water

Denholm

Hawick

Rubers Law △

Jed Water

Amble

Ettrick Water

Scottish Middle March

Cauldcleuch Head △

Kale Water

Redeswire Fray

R Coquet

offat

Peel Fell △

Otterburn

Rothbury

Boreland

Hermitage Castle

Deadwater

R Rede

Elsdon

TARRAS MOSS

Kielder Water

Otterburn

English Middle March

Dryfe Water

Langholm

Newcastleton

R North Tyne

Morpeth

Newbiggin-by-the-Sea

Lockerbie

Water of Milk

Gillesbie Tower

BEWCASTLE WASTE

Bellingham

Bedlington

Ashington

Ecclefechan

Liddel Water

Canonbie

ENGLAND

Cramlington

Blyth

Annan

Gretna

R Esk

Longtown

Bewcastle

Thirlwall Castle

Chollerford

NEWCASTLE upon TYNE

Tynemouth

TH

Solway Moss

R Irthing

Gilsland

Haltwhistle

Corbridge

South Shields

Annan

Debateable Land

Brampton

Hexham

R Tyne

Gateshead

illoth

Carlisle

English West March

R South Tyne

R Allen

Consett

Washington

Chester-le-Street

Sunderland

atria

Wigton

Dalston

R Caldrew

R Petteril

R Eden

Alston

Wearhead

Durham

Seaham

len

Bothel

Langwathby

Tow Law

Crook

Peterlee

Bassenthwaite Lake

Penrith

Cross Fell △

R Wear

Bishop Auckland

△ *Skiddaw*

R Lowther

Troutbeck

Appleby-in-Westmorland

Newton Aycliffe

Stockton-on-Tees

Keswick

mouth

Hartlepool

BATTLE VALLEYS

BATTLE VALLEYS
A PORTRAIT OF THE BORDER

Ronald Turnbull

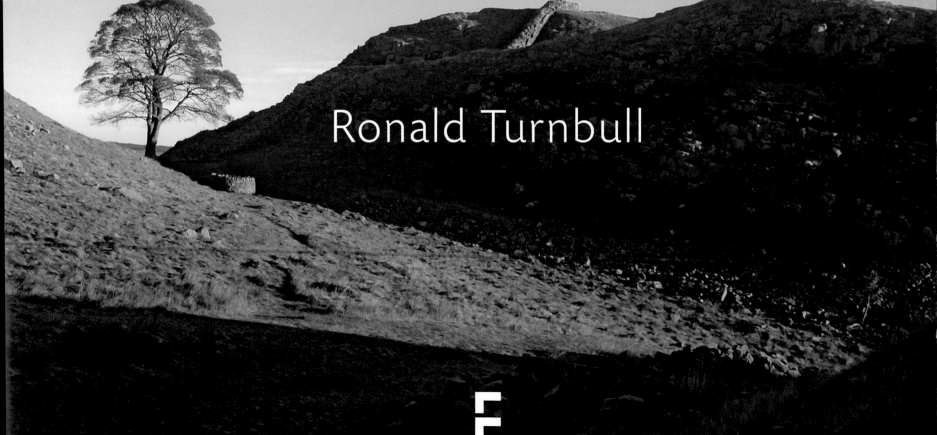

F

FRANCES LINCOLN LIMITED

PUBLISHERS

Frances Lincoln Limited
4 Torriano Mews
Torriano Avenue
London NW5 2RZ
www.franceslincoln.com

Battle Valleys
Text and photographs copyright © Ronald Turnbull 2012
Endpaper map contains Ordnance Survey data.
© Crown copyright and database right 2012

First Frances Lincoln edition: 2012

ISBN: 978-0-7112-3229-7

Printed and bound in China

9 8 7 6 5 4 3 2 1

HALF TITLE Lochmaben Castle. This is not the Bruce family
fortress, now a mere hump on the golf course, but one built
by England's King Edward I. It was captured by Scots from
English twice, by English from Scots once, and twice more by
the Scots king from local warlords.

TITLE PAGE Sycamore Gap, Hadrian's Wall, with the Wall itself
seen at top right.

THIS PAGE The farming lands of the East Marches were
described by Nigel Tranter as 'probably the most blood-
soaked in all these islands, acre for acre'. A tractor of today
spreads a more conventional organic manure.

CONTENTS

INTRODUCTION

I wish I could draw you over the Border in summer or
autumn, when we could at least visit some places in
that land where, though not very romantic in landscape,
every valley has its battle and every stream its song.

> Walter Scott, letter to Samuel Robertson, 1831

Our bloods have been cruelly shed, our goods be
opin depredation violentlie reft and spuilzied, and our
most plentifull and profitable roumes, for fear of their
incursions and oppressions, left desolat and desert,
without tennent or inhabitant.

> Treaty of the Kerrs, Scotts and others
> with King James VI and I, 1612

Bereived means raided, burnt out and starved to death.
For three hundred years, the country of the Border was
a little world between England and Scotland that had
its own laws, its own ethics, and an economy based on
theft, blackmail and kidnapping for ransom. Over moorland and bog, through the passes of Cheviot and the
fords of the Tyne, the reivers rode 60 miles in an autumn
night. A skirmish at dawn with lances and the long-shaft-
ed Jedburgh axe; then back again with the stolen cows,
and the smoke of burning thatch behind them.

A few miles from my home in Dumfriesshire, a pink
sandstone pile stands on the green banks of the River
Nith. Drumlanrig Castle is the seat (during the grouse
shooting season, at least) of the Duke of Buccleuch. He's
the UK's second largest landowner in terms of area, and
an intensely respectable fellow who speaks in the House
of Lords on organic farming, squirrels and the disabled.
His fortune is founded on stolen cows.

For the 'Bold Buccleuch', originally from Teviotdale
in the Scottish Middle March, was one of the most suc-
cessful of the border reivers. He was also one of the most
romantic, mounting a commando-type raid across the

border in 1596 to rescue Kinmont Willie from Carlisle Castle.

Among his henchmen on that exciting night there may well have been a Wattie Trummell or Tom Turnbull, subordinate neighbours from further down the Teviot. People sometimes ask me the meaning of my family name; but not in Northumberland, where it's obvious. In Hawick there's a statue commemorating the inaugural Turnbull, who gained name and lands by saving King Robert the Bruce from a nasty pair of horns. But that's a load of bull. Turnbulls too came raiding down across the Tyne during the three centuries of the lawless Border. The name celebrates success at the respected game of robbery – success enough to attract in 1510 the notice of King James IV himself.

> The clan of Turnbull having been guilty of unbounded excesses, the King came suddenly to Jedburgh, by a night march, and executed the most rigid justice upon the astonished offenders. Their submission was made with singular solemnity. Two hundred of the tribe met the King at the water of Rule, holding in their hands the naked swords with which they had perpetrated their crimes, and having each around his neck the halter which he had well merited. A few were capitally punished, many imprisoned, and the rest dismissed after they had given hostages for their future peaceable demeanour.
>
> Walter Scott, citing Holinshed's *Chronicle*.

Five hundred years ago, this green farmland of Nithsdale was a battleground. Warlords Maxwell and Johnstone burnt each other's villages, and engaged in pitched battle for the position of Provost of Dumfries.

Hadrian's Wall, looking east from Peel Crags.

And if the business of mutual slaughter did get in the way of the harvest, then it was off across the Debateable Land to raid the fields of Cumbria. The Scottish West March even had its own distinctive sword-slash. The Lockerbie Lick was a downward backhander delivered by a man on horseback towards the head of an enemy on foot.

It was a lifestyle that's been compared with that on the North-West Frontier of Afghanistan. It extended from Peebles to the gates of Newcastle, from Berwick to Kirkcudbright. As order and civilisation break down, it makes as much sense to go out and steal from your neighbour as to stay honestly at home until your neighbour comes and steals from you. The cattle-thieving, camel-thieving or horse-thieving culture is the same all over the world and throughout history. Its loyalty is not to any nation state or religion, but to the family and the tribe. Blackmail and kidnapping are honourable professions, and inter-clan relations are organised around the blood-feud.

Bellingham is a quiet country town with three pubs, a convenient Co-op and a phone box. I once left my wallet with £50 in cash in the phone box, and came back to find a polite gentleman searching through it for my address. But in 1597, Walter Scott of Harden raided Bellingham with 300 horsemen, heading north with household goods and 400 cattle. The following year the victims themselves turned raider, bringing home 300 beasts from Liddesdale.

North of the village, bog grasses run for a dozen miles into the foothills of Cheviot. In pubs around Otterburn the soldiers relax after hard days driving tanks across the brown moorland. But in August 1388, this was the scene of the greatest of the Border battles. James, 2nd Earl of Douglas, raided out of Scotland with 8,000 men. Returning with their stolen cattle, they were pursued by the local warlord on the English side, Henry Percy, Duke of Northumberland.

The Border ballad is cold, cruel, and yet stirs the blood like the wind across the Cheviot moors:

> There was ne'er a time on the March-parties
> Since the Douglas and Percie met,
> But it was marvail if the blood ran not
> As the rain doth run in the street.

According to the ballad, nobody on either side surrendered or ran away. Of the combined armies, just seventy-three English and fifty-five Scots survived. The fifty-five Scots had the better of it, coming away with prisoners worth 200,000 francs in ransom.

In 1603, the crowns of Scotland and England were united under King James VI and I. But the memory of the terrible centuries lingers on. Every valley boasts its 'bastle' or fortified farmhouse, its pele tower or grim border fortress. Ettrick and Yarrow, Liddesdale and Redesdale, Teviot and Tweed, lie almost empty now. Only the fierce little border towns survive: Melrose and Jedburgh and Galashiels, with their tough rugby and their horseback common-riding ceremonies. The green hollows of the hills, which were once 'passage and bye way for the theefe', lie empty under the wind. A sheep wanders through, and then another sheep, and after a few days a solitary hill walker, sleeping bag wrapped in green nylon against the dew.

Half past five on a November morning: still dark, but the reivers' moon is riding high. Socks that had been slightly damp the night before were now rigid, resisting my incoming toes as if made of stout cardboard.

ABOVE Hermitage Water, a branch of Liddesdale in the Scottish Middle March.

RIGHT Drumlanrig Castle, Nithsdale. If its owner, the Duke of Buccleuch, is the UK's largest private landowner in terms of area, this is down to the successes of his ancestors, the leading cattle thieves of the Scottish Middle March.

ABOVE Fieldhead, above Charlton, in Tynedale. The Charltons of the North Tyne were among the most effective reivers on the English side of the Border.

RIGHT Fatlips Castle, above the Teviot, was the pele tower stronghold of Turnbull of Bedrule.

LEFT St Mary's Loch, passed on a November morning on a walk across the Scottish West and Middle Marches.

BELOW Rising from the plains of the Tweed, the triple-topped Eildon Hills can be seen along most of the Border. This view, taken at 10pm on a summer night, is from Hownam Law, a Cheviot foothill on the Scottish side.

I hadn't taken my boots to bed with me as I'm a bit fussy about my bedmates. Stored in the rucksack, they'd stiffened up as well – but they would still admit feet. My water bottle, even though I had taken it into the bivvybag, rattled with a slush of ice. I did not linger over breakfast. I managed to get my boots tied just before my fingertips froze and became useless.

At the ridge end, the sky still showed stars above but paled to turquoise and flared orange along the hilltops. Only Nature herself could have the effrontery for such a colour scheme. Down along the shadowy Loch of the Lowes, the flashing light of an early gritter was like a spark dropped out of the sunrise. The sun itself came at 8 am on a low hill called Ward Law. Here shepherds have built tall, fanciful cairns, marking particularly suitable spots to see their sheep from. The low sun turned the moorland into a texture of tussocks, with a fluffed-out fox hunting nose-down after voles. In the valley below, a pele tower rose out of the pastel green of frosted fields, and each tree stood out as if drawn with a scratchy pencil.

Ettrick and Yarrow lost their people during the reiving years. Every ten or twenty minutes a car with misted windows zipped along the A708, but the black cows just carried on staring across the green slopes. Below the sky and the hills, St Mary's Loch lay in a haze of mist. Grasses were white against black ice like a photo in negative. Ahead lay the moors and swelling hills of Peeblesshire, with the Tweed beyond and buzzards mewing high above.

Along the Tweed, thickets of hogweed spring tall as reivers' lances, and the fields are splashed with lurid gorse, the colour of road-menders' jackets. Every ten miles the river passes another abbey broken down by the Earl of Hertford in the Border wars. A tractor trundles across a wide green field with an arc of brown slurry rising into the sunlight. Above are bleak moorlands, and the wild high Cheviot hills. Every fifth hill has a hill fort, picked out in yellow grasses by the low autumn sunlight. The curlew cries across the moors, and behind everything, the triple top of Eildon rises pale against a sky the pale blue of starlings' eggs.

Three hundred years of killing . . . and the result today is the most intensely peaceful part of our United (as it now is) Kingdom.

RIGHT Hole Bastle, near Bellingham. The bastle, or fortified farmhouse, served the same purpose as the pele tower on a smaller scale.

FAR RIGHT This small road at Deadwater, between Kielder and the head of Liddesdale, is the only road crossing of the Border in 25 miles between Kershopefoot in Liddesdale and Carter Bar.

Nithsdale and Dumfries

In the Middle Ages, Galloway was probably the most prosperous part of Scotland. Its mild climate supported rich farmland, it had a string of fishing villages and a lucrative pilgrimage site at Whithorn, all in a corner away from the politics and associated warfare of the Central Belt. Galloway as its name suggests had more affinity with Ireland, and even across the Solway with England.

The border of Galloway was the River Nith, flowing to the sea at Dumfries. The Scottish West March extended into Galloway: there was a minor international incident at Kirkcudbright in 1547, celebrated for the transaction (in Border terms, an utterly sensible one) whereby a good wife of the town handed her husband to the enemy for safekeeping, to be ransomed back after the battle.

The westernmost pele tower still standing is at Orchardton, 20 miles west of the river. Even so, for most reiving bands the crossing of the Nith was a ford too far. The risk was being trapped against the river on the return journey – exactly what happened to Sir Thomas Carleton, returning from that raid against Kirkcudbright with 2,000 sheep, 200 cattle and some horses. He found himself obliged to abandon the sheep . . . and so the edge of Galloway is, in a real sense, the beginning of the Border.

Standing astride what we could thus call the border of the Border is the burgh of Dumfries. Given a significant knife-fight that happened here in 1306, it's a convenient place to survey the history of Scotland in the time 'before the Borders'.

William of Normandy brought the feudal system to England. The baron lived in his castle, other aristocrats were ranged above him upwards to the king, and downwards as knights and squires – and everybody else was a peasant slave. Over the early Middle Ages this convenient system was adopted by successive Kings of Scotland, replacing, everywhere south of the Highlands, the ancient confusion of clans and local warlords. And so, every dozen miles on both sides of the Border, we see a Norman-style motte-and-bailey castle. Well, we see the motte, or ditch; the bailey, or fortress, was to be wrecked during the Border troubles and their return to the older clan-and-warlord political system.

Under the feudal system, you were a monk or priest, or else you were a strayed slave and could be put to death on sight. The Middle Class was, officially, illegal. The way around this was the Royal burghs. As well as the privilege of not being put to death, townsmen could wall themselves in, levy tolls, and govern their own affairs. They were entitled, and indeed obliged, to carry arms on their town's behalf, and they paid taxes directly to the King. Burghs across the Border included Carlisle, Selkirk, Kelso (an abbey burgh rather than a Royal one), Jedburgh and Berwick. They were strong enough to survive and even thrive through the times of the reivers. At Redeswire Fray, it was not some late-arriving warlord who decided the battle. It was the town of Jedburgh, with its dreaded war cry 'Jeddart's here!'

In 1386 Dumfries became one of the earliest Royal burghs, and, as the gateway to Galloway, it would be one of the most lively. Its stone bridge of 1431 was the longest in Europe – the Forth Road Bridge of its time. The original wooden footbridge was gifted to the town by Devorgilla, widow of the baron John Balliol. In his memory she also founded Balliol College at Oxford and Sweetheart Abbey, 8 miles south of Dumfries.

An oddity of Scotland's War of Independence is that Scotland had only been non-independent for about eight years. After King Alexander III, who died by falling from his horse, the Scots invited a particularly robust king of England, Edward I, to sort out who should come next. Edward, obviously, installed a harmless puppet of his own, John Balliol, the son of Devorgilla the bridge-builder, who for his uselessness was nicknamed Toom Tabard, or Empty Coat.

The candidates for the job of ousting Toom Tabard included Baron John Comyn (or Cummins), the Red Comyn, from Badenoch; and Robert de Brus, or Bruce, feudal lord of Annandale, whose family were Norman imports from England. The two met in the sanctuary of Greyfriars Church, Dumfries, to decide who should have first run for the Crown, in a forerunner of the Blair–Brown meeting of 1994 in Islington's Granita Restaurant. The outcome was different, however, as the Bruce–Comyn meeting developed into a knife fight in which the Red Comyn was killed.

Straightforward murder wouldn't have mattered, but murder in a church limited Bruce's future. His only chance was to get himself crowned king straight away, before the news of his wicked deed could reach the Pope and the order excommunicating him from the Church could get back to Scotland. He went on to lose small battles all over Scotland, before his final victory at Bannockburn, outside Stirling, in 1314.

ABOVE Caerlaverock Castle, a Maxwell stronghold south-east of Dumfries, protected by marshes as well as its moat. Even so, it was taken by siege by Edward I in 1300 and besieged again by the Scots during the War of Independence.

RIGHT Devorgilla Bridge, Dumfries: the Forth Road Bridge of the late Middle Ages.

During the Wars of Independence, Dumfries was burned down by the English on seven separate occasions. The crucial knife fight in Greyfriars Kirk was commemorated by a plaque above the freezer cabinet in Wm. Low's grocery. The building, opposite the modern Greyfriars Church (1867), is currently Blockbuster Video, where assuredly you can rent yourself a copy of *Braveheart*.

Bruce had no direct heir, so Scotland was ruled by a succession of Stewarts, all called James and numbered I to VI. The first three had the advantage that neighbour England was occupied with its own internal battles during the Wars of the Roses. Even so, times were not altogether easy, as can be summarised in the fates of the Jameses. James I was murdered in his privy in an attempted coup (the coup failed, and the plotters were intricately tortured to death by James's widow Queen Joan); James II was blown up in the Borders while supervising the siege of Roxburgh Castle outside Kelso; and James III died at the Battle of Sauchieburn, during a civil war against supporters of his son.

By this time the Wars of the Roses were over, and England was ready once again to dominate the Scots. So James IV died like his grandfather in the Borders, at the Battle of Flodden in 1513.

James V died of misery after the humiliating defeat by the English at Solway Moss, near Longtown. Mary Queen of Scots visited Hermitage Castle, in the Scottish Middle March, for an ill-judged but romantic rendezvous with her lover, James Earl of Bothwell. She was deposed aged only twenty-four in favour of her infant son James VI. And on the death of Queen Elizabeth in 1603, James became King James I of England.

During those 200 years between Scotland's crushing defeat at Flodden and the union of the two crowns under James VI and I, the Borders were the lawless buffer zone between the two kingdoms.

Today, despite the arrival of a micro-university (an outpost of Paisley) and the successes of its Queen of the South football team, Dumfries is in decline: it is less lively than at any time since the Dark Ages. In 1990 the town centre was bypassed and pedestrianized. During the first decade of the 2000s not one but two Tesco supermarkets colonised the ring road, along with other out-of-town emporia. So while the Council Offices in Irish Street did their bit (in 1986) to bring ugliness into the town, its old centre is likely to remain much as it is, an unselfconscious mix of red stonework from the Middle Ages to Georgian.

ABOVE Dumfries Tesco in lyrical evening light.

BELOW Nithsdale at Thornhill.

ROBERT BURNS

Burns was not a true Borderer, being a ploughboy from Alloway in Ayrshire. He did however pass through the Borders on his way to and from Edinburgh, stopping only to chat up some Border lass.

But with prosperity he became a Nithsdale farmer. While living at Ellisland, he disgraced himself by re-enacting a romantic episode from Classical history, the Rape of the Sabine Women – with his neighbour's daughters in the Sabine roles. When, as any poet farmer would, he became bankrupt and exhausted, his friends found him a job in the excise office in Dumfries. Here he lived in a small house in Stinking Vennel (since renamed Bank Street) and then in Mill Street (renamed Burns Street – with the cultured and broadminded Doonhamers renaming an intersecting street after Shakespeare).

In 1796 he died in Dumfries, aged thirty-seven. Given that he could seduce no more Dumfriesshire lasses and spring no more political rants in favour of the French Revolution, he could now safely be adopted as the national poet. Accordingly his bones were dug up from their pauper's grave and reburied under an impressive mausoleum in St Michael's churchyard – which is also notable for its bourgeois excesses of funerary art, inspired by the easily-worked Permian red sandstone.

The Burns Mausoleum, St Michael's Church.

Permian sandstone, mostly formed from desert dunes, forms the floors of Nithsdale and Annandale and colours Annan's High Street.

Annandale

East of the Nith, we're in true Border country. The layout of the Scottish West March did, however, restrict the reiving. Nith, Annan and Esk run parallel southwards; Nithsdale and Annandale run down to populated country and the sea, with no convenient raiding route into England.

The Nith was the Maxwells' land. Maxwells of Caerlaverock Castle served as West March Wardens, and the name is still common among the glen's farming families. Geography restricted their deadly enemies to the Johnstones, who dominated the Annan. Scotland's most lethal clan battle was not anywhere in the Highlands: it was the Maxwells against the Johnstones at the Sands of Dryfe in 1593. Their dispute started with the stealing of a single black horse at Gretna by one Willie Johnstone of Kirkhill. It continued with an army of 2,000 Maxwells being ingeniously ambushed by just 400 Johnstones. Seven hundred of the Maxwells were killed, some burned to death within the sanctuary of Lochmaben Kirk.

Lochmaben, at the foot of Annandale, was the lowest crossing of River Annan for those who didn't want to brave the tidal sands of the Solway. Here was the castle of the Bruce family, strategically sited between three lochs. The strongest fortress in the Borderland, its remains now form a small obstacle for golfers. For a summary of Lochmaben in the 1530s, we can turn to the chronicler Bellenden: 'Ane loch namit Lochmabern fyve mylis of length and foure of breid, full of uncouath fische' with inhabitants 'quhais cruelteis wes so gret that thay abhorrit nocht to eit the fllesche of yolding prisoneris. The wyvis usit to slay thair husbandis quhen thay were found cowartis or disconfist be thair ennymes, to give occasioun to utheris to be more bald & hardy' [quhais = whose; eit = eat; yolding = surrendering; quhen = when; disconfist = discomforted; bald = bold].

That uncouth fish, the vendace, is a survivor from the Ice Age. Originally a saltwater fish, it got cut off in inshore waters and adapted as the water gradually transformed from seawater to fresh. About the size of a herring, it also looks like a herring with a greenish back, but is actually a sort of small salmon. It is threatened by competing species such as roach and ruffe, arriving as live bait thrown in by anglers, and by silting of the gravel beds where it spawns. Farm fertiliser and sewage run-off enrich the water, encouraging the wrong sort of plankton. However, the most serious damage has been from rising water temperatures caused by global warming.

The last Lochmaben vendace was found inside the stomach of a pike, in the 1970s. The lakes are now too soupy to sustain it, even if it were reintroduced. The vendace has been established in Loch Skeen, at the head of the Grey Mare's Tail waterfall above Moffatdale. And cannibalism? Like the vendace, that assuredly no longer happens in Lochmaben.

FAR LEFT Lochmaben's main street features this statue of Robert the Bruce. The town hall was built in 1878.

LEFT Lochmaben Castle Loch, with a view to Burnswark, a hill fortified by the Romans for siege warfare practice.

GILLESBIE TOWER

Boreland is a cluster of stone houses on the hill road between Lockerbie and Eskdalemuir. I parked at its village hall, next to the recycling bins, and walked up a farm track alongside the Dryfe Water. In a patch of scrub between the track and the river, a few stones rise out of the brambles, the remains of Gillesbie Tower. It's a former stronghold of the Graham family, just one of dozens between Annan Water and the Esk. This one is notable because Sir Walter Scott happened to record a story about it.

In the reign of Charles I, thirty years after the end of the reiving times, his Grace the Earl of Traquair (who was at the time the Lord High Treasurer) mentioned to his friend Christie's Will Armstrong that he was about to lose a case at the Court of Session. Christie's Will discovered that the court's president, Lord Durie, was in the habit of riding out at dusk across Leith Links on the outskirts of the city. It was the work of an instant to snatch the judge from his horse, bind him tightly in his own cloak, and carry him across the hills to Gillesbie Tower. Here they shut him into the vault below the castle.

Each day food was passed to the poor Lord Durie through a hole in the door. All he heard was the wind, and the river, and each day a weird voice that cried: 'Batty!' and another that cried 'Maudge!' Naturally enough, he concluded that he had suddenly died on Leith Links, and was now in Hell, Batty and Maudge being the resident demons.

Without a judge, the court case collapsed. A few weeks later the miserable man was seized in his sleep, re-wrapped in his cloak, and returned to Leith Links. He vowed to improve his conduct in life and for years dined out on his dreadful experience of being seized by demons. Then one day he happened to pass along the Dryfe Water – and heard a farm woman calling to her cat Maudge, and the shepherd's dog called Batty.

RIGHT Graham Tower at Gillesbie, Boreland, and the remains of the hellish underground cell inhabited by Lord Durie.

Eskdale

Upper Eskdale was the country of the Elliots (also spelt Eliot, Eliott, but never Elliott), while the Armstrongs held the lower valley south of Langholm. The Armstrongs were probably the most dangerous of all the tribes, and were (possibly still are) at deadly feud with, among many others, the Turnbulls. They also dominated the Debateable Lands and the dreaded dale of the Liddel Water, so will be descending out of the Tarras Moss into the later chapters of this book.

The Armstrong clan museum is in the grey stone town of Langholm, hemmed in by hills and divided by the silver Esk. But more notable than any Eskdale murderer or cattle thief was a farm urchin born 200 years after the union of the crowns.

Nor pass the tentie curious lad,
Who o'er the ingle hangs his head,
And begs of neighbours books to read;
For hence arise
Thy country's sons, who far are spread,
Baith bold and wise.
[tentie = attentive; ingle = fireplace corner]
Verse addressed to Burns by Thomas Telford

The Scots have a name for such folk: they are 'lads o' pairts'. Ever since John Knox decreed that all should read and write so that they could read the Bible, Scotland has had a respect for education. And so, in every generation, a handful of young men from the fields and the back streets would get hold of the books, and read themselves into the

Terraced houses, Langholm

LEFT A grey heron in the Esk matches the town's stonework.

BELOW LEFT The library endowed by Langholm lad Thomas Telford.

BELOW RIGHT Spontaneous sculpture on Whita Hill above Langholm.

intellectual life of the country. Robert Burns, the Ayrshire ploughboy, is one example. But perhaps this tendency was strongest in the Borders, among the tough, and tough-minded, descendents of the reiving times.

Out of Ecclefechan in Annandale came Thomas Carlyle, born in 1795 the son of a stonemason. He walked across the Borders to Edinburgh University, and eventually became the leading historian and philosopher of his age, publishing in 1830 a long and passionate social history of the French Revolution.

Explorer David Livingstone was born at Blantyre in Lanarkshire, and at the age of ten was working in the cotton mills there. In true Scottish tradition the mill owner offered his child labourers free schooling at the end of their twelve-hour working day. Mungo Park, in his time an equally famous explorer in Africa, was born in 1771 in the Yarrow valley, the seventh child of a tenant farmer. The next glen northwards bred James Hogg, the Ettrick Shepherd, novelist and journalist and, after the death of Robert Burns, Scotland's leading poet.

But none started so low as the illegitimate son of a dairymaid in Eskdale. Thomas Telford, known as 'laughing Tam', was born at Westerkirk near Langholm in 1757. As soon as he was old enough he was sent out to neighbouring farms to herd sheep. As with David Livingstone, his employers worked him hard and paid him not much, but allowed him the liberty of the library. Aged fourteen he was apprenticed to a stonemason, and at the age of twenty-three left Eskdale to help build Edinburgh's New Town. Two years later he was working at Portsmouth docks.

'As knowledge is my most ardent pursuit a thousand things occur which call for investigation which would pass unnoticed by those who are content to trudge only in the beaten path,' he wrote. By the end of his career he had mastered bridge construction in stone (Pontcysyllte aqueduct), cast iron (Craigellachie) and wrought iron (the Menai suspension bridge). He built the Caledonian Canal right along Scotland's Great Glen, and 900 miles of roads and bridges in the Scottish Highlands. At the end of his life he left to Langholm a handsome stone library of 6,000 volumes.

Below Langholm the Esk is joined by a major tributary from the East, the Liddel. Liddesdale, the stronghold of the Armstrongs, may be part of the Solway water system but its hill passes lead immediately into Tynedale and Teviot, and it was counted as part of the Scottish Middle March. Joined with Liddel Water, the Esk then runs into the coastal plain, to mark the Scotland–England border.

Or does it? Twelve miles of land, between the Esk and the Sark, belonged neither to England nor to Scotland, but to the Armstrongs entirely. This, the Debateable Land, deserves a chapter all of its own.

A more formal artwork commemorates Langholm's poet,
Hugh Macdiarmid, who wrote in sturdy Border Scots.

2 THE DEBATEABLE LAND

Between the Sark burn to the north, and the River Esk to the south, a strip of land 4 miles wide and 12 long belonged to neither England nor Scotland – or else, if you wanted to look at it that way, to both. The convenient consequence was that neither kingdom could assert its authority there without an international incident. Scots and English equally were allowed to graze cattle and sheep in the Debateable Land during the day – it was, and is, a fertile bit of farmland. But nobody was to make a permanent settlement, or graze cattle or sheep overnight.

Nevertheless it was inhabited, by Elliots and Armstrongs. 'Elliots and Armstrongs ride thieves all,' but as Walter Scott notes, 'to what Border family of note would not such an adage have been equally applicable?' It was certainly applicable to the Grahams, a family technically English but in practice international.

Longtown in England and Gretna in Scotland both overlook the Debateable Land. The small town of Canonbie is squarely inside it, making a nonsense of the 'no settlement' rule. Also making a nonsense of that rule, as well as any others that interfered with the convenience of the no-nation enclave, was Johnie Armstrong, 'Black Jock' of Gilnockie. It was said that he levied protection money from the Border right across to Newcastle.

In the summer of 1530, the teenage King James V made an expedition through the borders. Johnie Armstrong proudly came out to meet him with thirty-six riders at Carlenrig Chapel, 10 miles south of Hawick on the road to Langholm.

> When Johnie cam before the King,
> Wi' a' his men sae brave tae see,
> The King he movit his bonnet to him;
> He ween'd he was a King as well as he.

James understood only too well Johnie's local sovereignty: 'What wants [lacks] that knave that a king should have?' – and ordered him and the thirty-six riders to be hanged on nearby trees. Johnie understood this

BELOW After 500 years, Armstrongs still practice cattle relocation in the Debateable Land. This view across the Esk shows the Armstrong Mart at Longtown, one of the biggest in Northern England. Meanwhile, the small department store in Haltwhistle is Armstrong-owned. Its bridal department offers 'the Armstrong Touch' – presumably these days not involving a twelve-foot lance and a lethal head wound.

RIGHT Clochmaben Stone stands on the shoreline at Gretna. Originally part of a Neolithic stone circle, it was used as a meeting point on days of Border truce.

Gretna's first and last house, a few steps from the Border, is the original Marriage Room where runaway couples from England could get married under Scots law; competing Original Marriage Rooms are in the (two) Old Blacksmith's Shops.

as simply the first bid in a haggle over ransom, and responded with an offer of twenty-four milk-white steeds, as much English gold as four of them could carry, twenty-four working corn mills, twenty-four fighting nephews for James's army, and the rents of middle Liddesdale.

When James turned down the offer, Johnie upped his bid: he'd bring the King any English subject up to the rank of Duke, dead or alive. James rightly felt that Black Jock dead was worth more than any English duke alive.

On his way to the gallows, Johnie pointed out that he was an even worse enemy to Henry VIII than he was to his own king. 'Had I known, Sir, that you would have taken my life this day, I should have lived on the borders in spite of King Harry and you both, for I know King Harry would down-weigh my best horse with gold to know that I were condemned to die this day.'

Black Jock's end shows the peculiar richness of the Border history. His ballad 'Johnie Armstrong' was passed from mouth to ear for 200 years before being collected by Sir Walter Scott. But we also have the chronicles written at the time, and even invoices for rope used to hang the reivers.

The ballads not only recorded history but in their small way also made it. When Henry VIII invaded Scotland in 1542, one of his reasons was the 'dispiteful and slanderous balladis' about him, possibly dealing with his marital affairs. Not that Henry needed reasons to invade Scotland, and if he did, there was always the latest raid out of Liddesdale. In that autumn of 1542 the English army mustered at Berwick, raiding and burning into the Scottish Middle March. Kelso and Roxburgh were burned down, not for the first or last time.

In response to that ballad-induced raid, James sent his army south-westwards through the hills to attack in the far west. (Two hundred and three years later his descendant, Bonnie Prince Charlie, would pull off the same strategic coup.) The result would be the Battle of Solway Moss, the only conflict of actual armies within the Debateable Lands. The English West March Warden, Lord Wharton, was at Carlisle with 300 Border horsemen. He led those horsemen north to harry the army. They were absurdly few, but knew the country in detail and were, as George MacDonald Fraser describes them, 'the finest irregular light cavalry in Europe'.

Meanwhile, James's army was suffering a crisis of command. Its leader, the Borderer and Scottish West March Warden Lord Maxwell, had just been supplanted by a Royal favourite, Oliver Sinclair. We can only specu-late as to why King James had granted Sinclair such authority, or why Sinclair chose that particular moment to exercise it. Scots Military history is mostly disasters – 'In five hundred years the number of decisive battles won against the English could be counted on one hand, leaving a finger or two to wag in caution,' is how John Prebble puts it.

But of all those disasters, Solway Moss was the most humiliating. With confusion at its head, and trapped against the marshes and wide fords of the Esk River, the Scots army fell to pieces. Scots knights were surrendering in groups to single English riders, and even to local women. A total of 1,200 Scots were taken prisoner. Lord Maxwell himself was taken by one George Forster, who presumably retired in comfort on the ransom. Battle casualties were astonishingly low. Wharton estimated seven deaths on his own side, and twenty Scots, though many more Scots drowned in the Esk and Line Rivers.

If the English Borderers were the most effective of light cavalry, so too were the Borderers on the Scottish side. Did they play no part in the battle? They did indeed. As the broken Scots army limped its way home through the hills, the Armstrongs and Elliots descended out of Liddesdale, killing and looting. There were plenty of Elliots and Armstrongs, and they inflicted far more casualties than Wharton and his English riders.

With this particular bout of warfare over and the ransoms all paid, it seemed a good time to settle the nuisance of the Debateable Land. As a preliminary, the inhabitants were encouraged to relocate by an agreement that anyone, of either nation, should be free to commit any crime whatsoever within its 40 square miles. Lord Maxwell followed up in 1551 by raiding the area and destroying every building.

Finally, in 1522, the French Ambassador was invited to draw a line across the map. He gave the Scots the eastern and larger share. From the Scots point of view though, the English had all the decent land, with the Scots getting mostly moor. So each side considered the settlement unfair on itself; but each side, grudgingly, agreed that a bad, unfair settlement was better than no settlement at all. The ambassador's line was marked, and still is, by a ditch and earthwork known as the Scots Dyke.

But the debate rumbles on. In 1861, the builders of the Waverley rail line from Carlisle to Edinburgh avoided an awkward bend by rerouting the River Esk – ignoring the international repercussions of their act. And in 2002 the purchaser of Riddings Farm, on the English side of the river, was dismayed at having to pay two separate sets of conveyancing fees. Two acres of his farm, on the English side of the Esk River, turned out to be in Scotland.

TOP The Scot's Dyke was raised in 1552 to divide the Debateable Land between the kingdoms. It survives here and there below the trees of a narrow plantation.

ABOVE Hollows Tower, an Armstrong stronghold, stands above River Esk north of Canonbie. It's sometimes taken as the Gilnockie Tower of Black Jock, but the original Gilnockie Tower was larger, stood a half-mile downstream, and was destroyed by Lord Dacre the English West March Warden, once Johnie himself had been hanged.

Longtown's main street runs directly to the Esk Bridge, leading
all the traffic of the A7 through the heart of the town.

Longtown has turned through 90 degrees; its former main street, Nith Place, runs down to the ford over the Esk River. The river at this point is bottomed not with stones and boulders but with Permian sandstone bedrock, making for a comfortable crossing for man or horse whenever the river is reasonably low.

The main difference in the landscape from 500 years ago is land drainage. At the time of Solway Moss, we have to imagine the river even wider and bordered by bog. In the battle, the river took many more Scots lives than Wharton's 300 riders did.

Carlisle

The English West March is more or less commensurate with modern-day Cumbria. This is confusing to those of us who believe the regional slogan: 'Cumbria: the Lake District'. Lakeland, which had been so open to the Viking raiders, was protected from the worst of the Border lawlessness. It is harder to drive cattle over Scarth Gap than the moorlands of Bewcastle Waste or the grassy Southern Uplands.

Even so, legend records one raid into the fastnesses of Borrowdale by the reiving Graeme (or Graham) family. The men of Borrowdale were organised into a pursuit, or 'hot trod', after the raiders. To protect their escape with the slow-moving cattle, the Grahams set an ambush below Honister Crags. The leaders on both sides were killed in the battle.

Aside from its craggy rocks, the other reason for Lakeland's comparative safety was the fortress city of Carlisle, which stood right across the route any raiders would be taking home with the stolen cattle.

Carlisle's 2,000 years of history are hidden in odd corners, or rebuilt in Victorian brick. This was a crucial river crossing and Roman fort even before the building of Hadrian's Wall; but Carlisle's surviving Roman remains are stored on shelves in the Tullie House Museum. Carlisle's medieval vennels (alleyways) have been roofed over and rebuilt as their twenty-first-century equivalent, a shopping mall. Two Victorian red-stone towers opposite the station refer vaguely to the south gate of the original walled town.

The twelfth-century cathedral is masked by smaller buildings around it. The fine Jacobean House (just the one survives) is enclosed within the redbrick walls of Tullie House Museum. The redbrick Debenhams building has a lorry-sized service entrance oddly

LEFT Carlisle Castle seen across its former moat

BELOW Carlisle Market Square and Moot Hall

Carlisle Castle, two thousand years of military history and the key to the West Marches.

ABOVE Inside the Half-Moon Battery, built to protect the gateway to the Inner Ward of the castle in the 1540s as part of the upgrade for the gunpowder age. Three cannon were mounted above, while these loopholes command the inner moat and its approaches.

BELOW LEFT Armoured car and field gun from the Second World War outside the military museum.

BELOW RIGHT The sally port in the west wall allowed entry to the raid that rescued Kinmont Willie. It was then blocked in on both sides, the original oak door being uncovered again early in the twentieth century.

echoing Hermitage Castle, although the Debenhams version is even uglier. Even Carlisle's castle is away across a noisy dual carriageway. In the Middle Ages, the moat here had much the same separating effect.

A generation after the Norman invasion of England, William Rufus (son of William the Conqueror) built Carlisle Castle to dominate Cumbria. From then on it was besieged, captured, recaptured and enlarged on a regular basis. Its military history starts at the very beginning: an altar-stone from the Roman fort, carved by a Syrian soldier of the third century, was reused as a mantelpiece in the gatehouse.

From 1135 to 1157 the castle was occupied by the Scots, along with most of Cumbria. In 1216 the citizens handed it

over to the Scots as they were considered to be less oppressive than King John. The castle was recaptured by a formal sit-down siege. It was besieged again during the Scottish Wars of Independence by King Robert the Bruce, but his siege engines got stuck in the mud and the siege failed.

From 1380 on the castle was adapted to the new warfare of cannon and musket. The walls and even the keep were lowered and thickened, giving the castle its unromantic squat outline. The next attack was in 1537, during the popular uprising against Henry VIII known as the Pilgrimage of Grace.

During the English Civil War it was besieged by the Scots under General Leslie, with the city and castle starved into submission after eight months. In 1745 it was captured and occupied by Bonnie Prince Charlie. In 1819 the military moved back in, and repaired it against the threat of socialist uprisings as the weavers of Carlisle paraded under its walls with such radical banners as 'Trial by Jury'. The castle was a military barracks right through the Second World War, when the roof of the keep carried an anti-aircraft gun.

Most significantly of all, during the reiving times it was the headquarters of the West March Warden, his prestigious home, and the key to the western Border. Reivers captured by the Warden were hanged on Haribee Hill (or, if funds were tight, more cheaply drowned in the River Eden).

In all the castle's 2,000 exciting years, the night of 13 April 1596, stands out. The story starts a few weeks earlier, with a day of truce at Kershopefoot at the eastern tip of the Debateable Land. William Armstrong of Kinmont rode home from the meeting along the Scottish bank of the Liddel Water, with the main group of English riders paralleling his course on their own side.

Kinmont Willie was a particularly notorious rogue. A few years before, along with Nebless Clem Croser and 300 followers, he'd raided Tynedale and lifted 1,300 cattle, burnt sixty houses, and killed ten men. But it was a day of truce, and under the March Laws the English riders couldn't touch him.

MacDonald Fraser suggests that, with the security of the day of truce, Willie may have made across the river some of 'those words and gestures which are such an eloquent currency in the West March to this day'. When the English riders sulked, he made a few more of the eloquent gestures. The English lost patience, found a ford across the river, and rode him down. Kinmont Willie was led captive to Carlisle Castle.

The West March Warden, Lord Scrope, was obliged under March Laws to release Willie immediately. But having got hold of such a notable villain he was reluctant to let him go. On the other hand, hanging him would undermine the March Laws and inflame the powerful Keeper of Liddesdale, Walter Scott of Buccleuch.

The Bold Buccleuch was pretty inflamed anyway.

> And have they taen him, Kinmont Willie
> Withouten either dread or fear?
> And forgotten that the bauld Buccleuch
> Can back a steed, or shake a spear?

And after writing several letters to Scrope pointing out his error, he decided the sword was simpler. He waited for a stormy night, and set out for Carlisle Castle with eighty riders. Two hours before dawn, they crossed the Eden at Stanwix, half a mile below the castle.

> We crept on knees, and held our breath
> Till we placed the ladders against the wa';
> And sae ready was Buccleuch himsell
> To mount the wa' before us a'.
>
> He's ta'en the watchman by the throat,
> He flung him down upon the lead –
> Had there not been peace between our lands,
> Upon the other side thou hadst gaed!

That's how the ballad has it. The true story is more complicated. To start with, the raiders had inside help. There were the English Grahams, through whose ground they'd ridden to Carlisle by an arrangement made at the Langholm horse races. But Buccleuch also had the nod from influential men within the castle – including Thomas Carleton, former deputy West March Warden. Carleton had been dismissed, he thought unfairly, by Scrope. He was a partner in various Graham blackmail rackets, and was also fulfilling a family obligation to Willie, who was a distant relative.

Nor was there any climbing of ladders or scaling of walls. The raiding party was in and out through the small sally port in the west wall – the one that now looks out over a pay-and-display car park. The trickiest bit was carrying the prisoner, still in his chains, back through the flooded River Eden. The two ambushes Buccleuch had set across the return route were not required as the garrison was in confusion and there was no pursuit.

Once across the Esk, at Dick's Tree, Buccleuch woke up the blacksmith with a lance point through his bedroom window. The smith's small daughter remembered the 'sair clatter' at the door, the horsemen wet in their armour in the grey of dawn, and Willie sitting side-saddle in his fetters, as recorded 230 years after the event by Walter Scott. The smithy was still open for business into the twentieth century, but since then has been remodelled and pebbledashed into ugliness.

Brampton

The old main road through Brampton bypasses its market square and High Street and the new main road, the A69, bypasses Brampton altogether. So it remains, as it has since the thirteenth century, a handsome market town made of red Penrith Sandstone. Green above the red stonework, the wooded Moat Hill, 60m (200 feet) high, gives no evidence, other than its name, of being a Norman motte.

Even the Border reivers tended to bypass Brampton, protected as it was by Naworth Castle, the stronghold of the Lords Dacre under their banner of the Red Bull, just 2 miles away.

There was one small skirmish here, in 1570, during the Revolt of the North against Queen Elizabeth in favour of Mary Queen of Scots. Crookback Leonard Dacre of Naworth, deputy Warden of the English West March, supported Mary and the old religion. Baron Hunsdon, Queen Elizabeth's cousin and Governor of Berwick, was hurrying from Hexham to join up with his allies at Carlisle, threatened as they were by an army of Humes, Kerrs and Scotts of the Scottish East and Middle Marches.

Dacre, with 3,000 men to Hundson's 1,500, didn't bother waiting for those powerful but perhaps untrustworthy Borderers. He ambushed Hunsdon where Hell Beck joins the River Gelt just south of the town. If Hunsdon had run, the UK today might be a Roman Catholic country, speaking Lowland Scots. But Hunsdon held his ground, and England was held for Queen Elizabeth.

Around 1600, the Grahams failed to burn down a house in Brampton containing the Land Sergeant at Gilsland, one John Musgrave. After this Brampton settled gently into becoming the quiet country town it still is today.

LEFT The stones of Lanercost tell a story spanning 1,500 years. Lanercost Priory, an Augustinian foundation of 1169, was founded by the Norman Robert de Vaux in atonement for the treacherous way he'd murdered his predecessor, the Celtic leader Gil, who gave his name to Gilsland. Stones for the priory were quarried from Hadrian's Wall, just half a mile to the north. Accordingly, no Hadrian remains lie along the 5-mile stretch past Lanercost. Edward I used Lanercost as his base for the war against Scotland, and the priory grew rich on Scottish loot. Robert the Bruce, once he'd defeated the English, partly destroyed the place. Its current state displays not one but two separate pele towers. One is incorporated into the main front of the home farm, the other (on the left of the picture) forms the corner of the cloisters.

ABOVE Brampton's main square and Moot Hall.

ABOVE RIGHT Possibly the UK's narrowest estate agent.

RIGHT Talkin Tarn lies two miles south of Brampton. Glacial moraines enclose it, and it's peculiar in having no stream running either in or out.

Bewcastle Waste

Now Hobbie was an English man,
In Bewcastle dale was bred and born:
But his misdeeds they were sae great,
They banish'd him ne'er to return.
                    Border ballad 'Jock o' the Side'

When you think of famous Cumbrians, they tend to be cultural chaps: the Wordsworths and Coleridge (OK, Coleridge was an incomer), Norman Nicholson, Melvyn Bragg and Adam Sedgwick the geologist. There was also one well-known comedian: Stan Laurel, of Laurel and Hardy fame, who was born in Ulverston.

You probably wouldn't think of Hobbie Noble. He too wandered lonely as a cloud, but this was only because he didn't want the West March Warden to find out where he was going. His cattle-thieving, blackmailing, and extortion were so effective that even his blackmailing, cattle-thieving neighbours had enough of him and drove him into Scotland. There he teamed up with the Armstrongs of Mangerton in the Debateable Land. They greatly appreciated his local knowledge of invading bits of England. And yet, like Wordsworth and Norman Nicholson, Hobbie Noble was a man of poetry. He is celebrated in stirring verse, in two separate Border ballads – 'Hobbie Noble' and 'Jock o' the Side'.

If you don't think of Hobbie Noble among the famous Cumbrians, that may be because his home is a bit you don't think of as Cumbria. Bewcastle Waste stretches, bleak and boggy, to the Scottish border and the shadowy plantations of Wark. I arrived from the north, crossing the Border by a bridge overhung by ancient oaks, on a road that dipped into tiny empty valleys. The occasional farm cottage stood on the slopes, but on a frosty autumn morning I passed nobody at all on the road.

That loneliness is only in the last five centuries. For the Romans, Bewcastle's high ground was the straight way into Scotland. Two of their signal stations stand on corners of the moor, linked by the Maiden Way, and where their road dipped into a moor-edge hollow they built a four-cornered fort. In Saxon times this was still a meeting of the ways, the equivalent of the M6 roundabout at the northern edge of Carlisle. Instead of motorway services they built a small church, with the carved Saxon cross-shaft which still stands in the churchyard.

The castle occupies the back corner of a farmyard, and cowpats now cover the Roman remains. Bewcastle has been ravaged by time – but also by the cattle thieves of Scotland. For the Armstrongs and Elliots on the Scottish side, and for the Nixons, Crosiers and another lot of Armstrongs on the English, the high, wide Bewcastle Waste, with its concealing knolls and obstructing bogs, was a main road back and forth across the Border.

TOP 'Passage and hy way for the theife': Bewcastle Waste, from just west of Bewcastle village.

ABOVE The Bew Castle, named for the Celtic Beugh, who built the original wooden castle. Improved in stone by the Norman Robert de Vaux, it became an important strong point in the reiving times. The Master of Bewcastle operated a semi-independent command under the West March Warden, interspersed with some freelance reiving on his own behalf.

All the mysguyded men, borderers of the same, inhabiting within Eskdale, Ewsdale, Walghopedale, Liddesdale, and a part of Tividale, foranempt Bewcastelldale, and a part of the middle marches of this the king's bordours, entres not this west and middle marches, to do any attemptate to the king our said soveraine's subjects: but thaye come throrow Bewcastelldale, and retornes, for the most part, the same waye agayne.

So complained Hunsdon's opponent Lord Dacre, Warden of the English West March, to Cardinal Wolsey in 1528.

The Captain of Bewcastle, stationed here with a troop of horse, formed a strongpoint guarding the raiders' passage through the moorland. Or he would have done if he hadn't been one of the main raiders himself.

Around Bewcastle, each farmhouse was built as a 'bastle', with space for cattle below and the main quarters reached by an internal trap door or an external stair. Bastles were strong enough to hold raiders off for a night, while neighbours could be gathered to help. The first farm I passed was Peel o' Hill – the name says it all. Just up the valley are the ruins of Hobbie's birthplace, Crew Castle. Near the road below is Hobbie Noble's Well, a spring with a falling rail fence around it.

When the Armstrongs needed to rescue their cousin Jock o' the Side from the castle at Newcastle, Hobbie was one of three chosen for the daring raid.

LEFT Saxon cross, Bewcastle church. It combines a Runic inscription with a Syrian-inspired figure of Christ the King. It and the similar Ruthwell Cross in Dumfriesshire are 'the greatest achievement of their date in the whole of Europe', according to Nikolaus Pevsner.

BELOW Hobbie Noble's Well – here 'well' has its earlier meaning of a natural spring.

> Thy coat is blue, thou hast been true,
> Since England banish'd thee to me.

Up on the moors, there's plenty of mud and marsh but a shortage of clean water for man or horse. It's easy to imagine Hobbie and his band stopping at this spring in the dark, on their journey across the high moors to the Choller ford on the Tyne. The raid resembles the rescue of Kinmont Willie from Carlisle except that there were only the three of them, they travelled about four times as far, and they didn't have traitors to help them at the other end.

Hobbie's two companions were both sons of Armstrong himself, Laird's Jock and Laird's Wat. They reversed their horseshoes to confuse pursuers, and disguised themselves as corn-caugers – ponymen carrying oats and barley. Once across the Tyne at Chollerford, they cut a tree 'wi fifteen nogs on either side' to use as a ladder. The tree turned out too short so they took the straightforward way, knifing the watchman.

Like Kinmont Willie, the rescued Jock suffers the indignity of riding side-saddle in his fetters like a woman.

> O Jock! sae winsomely's ye ride
> Wi' baith your feet upon ae side;
> Sae weel ye're harneist, and sae trig, [neat]
> In troth ye sit like ony bride!

They recross the Choller ford which is, as always on such expeditions, in spate. According to the ballad, the pursuing land sergeant stops on the bank of the Tyne, and asks for his valuable fetters back.

Behind Hobbie's Well a track leads up onto the moors. Watch Rigg, along with nearby Spy Rigg and Great Watch Hill, marks one of the nightly guard posts along the Border. You can walk all day here through

LEFT Cross-bedded gritstone on Crew Crag.

ABOVE Bew Castle and Peel o' Hill farm, with evening sun revealing traces of medieval field systems beyond the castle. The field behind and to left of the castle has been identified as a Medieval settlement.

BELOW Bewcastle Waste, looking north from Side Fell.

the confusing moorland that was 'passage and hye way for the theefe'. You'll see orange grasses, and a low cliff of gritstone, and then across miles of empty country the silver gleam of the Solway.

The tradition of quiet violence continues. White Preston Hill is an installation for electronic warfare. Around its high fence, signs warn of non-ionising radiation – radio or microwaves, but there's nothing you can do about them and they're probably harmless. A track leads through a corner of the Wark Forest which stretches from here to Kielder. I came out into clear-felled ground at a sign threatening me with arrest under the Official Secrets Act.

Spadeadam Range was a Cold War bunker for the Blue Streak nuclear missile. It's not so secret these days, as the RAF invites local running clubs to a Border Reivers half marathon within the grounds. Still, rather than getting arrested, it seemed best to turn aside to Barron's Pike, site of a Roman signal station.

Four miles further across the moor, 'the Beacon' has to be another lookout station. The map marks a second Roman signal station near by but neither it nor their road, Maiden's Way, is visible on the ground.

I come down to the church again at evening, peaty to the knees and exhausted. Crows circle over the ruined Bew Castle, and a tractor moves across a distant hill. Shadows gather in the churchyard, the one that it's said contains only the graves of women – Bewcastle menfolk ended up hanged at Carlisle. That was certainly the fate of Hobbie Noble. His glamour and success were not admired in England, but neither were they by some of the Armstrongs. When Sim of the Mains asked Hobbie to guide another Armstrong foray south into England, he betrayed his own raid to the English Warden. Hobbie Noble was captured, bound with his own bowstring, and hanged on Harrabee Hill.

Hobbie's patron, the Armstrong Laird of Mangerton, was not pleased to lose his useful Bewcastle guide. Sim fled to England, but his cousin knew plenty of bad things about him. All of these he passed on to the English, who strung Sim up on the same gallows that had hanged Hobbie.

So Wordsworth is all very well. But for a Cumbrian with a bit of blood and battle, remember Hobbie Noble of Bewcastle Waste.

4 SCOTTISH MIDDLE MARCH

Liddesdale

Of Liddisdail the commoun theifis

Sa peartlie steillis now and feifis,

That nane may keip

Horse, nolt nor scheip,

Nor yett dar sleip

For their mischeifis.

    Maitland's Complaynt, aganis the Thievis of Liddisdail

The gentle grassy hilltops where you're alone with the sky-larks and the sky; the glens with their small streams lively in the shadow of the alder trees: it's easy to forget the times of blood and fire which formed the Borders. Not, however, when that lively stream is the Liddel Water.

Along a border well stocked with murderous rogues, Liddesdale was counted as the worst. A visitor, finding no churches, asked 'Are there no Christians here?' 'Nah,' came the reply, 'we's a' Elliots and Armstrangs.'

Thirty peles of the Elliots rose out of Upper Liddesdale and Hermitage; there were even more Armstrong ones in Lower Liddesdale. The Liddel Water drains into the Esk, but the dale was subsumed into the Scottish Middle March as the reiver's high roads lead straight over the hills northwards into Teviotdale, and south or east over the convenient Bewcastle Waste into Tynedale.

But even within the Middle March, Liddesdale was a world apart. Like Bewcastle across the border, Liddesdale had its own Keeper who was more or less autonomous and based at the most intimidating, and the ugliest, of all

The head of Liddesdale, above Saughtree. Around 1580, this was the most dangerous place in all Scotland, inhabited by Armstrongs and the occasional Elliot.

the Border fortresses. Hermitage Castle was the posting in all the Border with the least scope for civilised behaviour. If its Keeper were anything less than a murderous warlord and gangmaster, he would be the wrong man for the job.

Fortunately, plenty of murderous warlords were available. Perhaps the worst (or, from the point of view of the English Middle March Warden, the best) was Sir William de Soulis the sorcerer, who died around 1318. His familiar, Robin Redcap, appeared as an old man with red eyes, taloned fingertips, and heavy iron boots. Robin's hat was coloured with the blood of his murdered victims, and, if the blood were to dry out, Redcap would die. (Despite his heavy boots, you can't outrun him. The trick is to quote any verse from the Bible.) King Robert received so many complaints about de

ABOVE Inside Hermitage Castle

BELOW Queen's Mire, high on the shoulder of Cauldcleuch Head

Soulis' spells and cruelties that he said: 'I don't care what you do with him, boil him in brew, but let me be plagued no more!' Taking the hint,

> They rolled him up in a sheet of lead –
> A sheet of lead for a funeral pall;
> They plunged him in a cauldron red,
> And melted him, lead and bones and all.

That's the ballad version. He actually plotted with the English against the king, forfeited the castle, and died a prisoner in Dumbarton.

Third-wickedest Master of Hermitage was James Hepburn, Earl of Bothwell. Bothwell was small but strong, ugly but sexy, intelligent and recklessly brave. In 1566 he attempted to arrest, on his own, Little Jock Elliot of the Park. He shot him out of the saddle, but when he approached to secure his prisoner, Elliot stabbed him three times. Bothwell was carried back to Hermitage in a cart, only to discover that some other Elliots already held captive there had taken over the place, and he had to negotiate with them to get back in.

Bothwell had loyally supported Mary Queen of Scots in the recent rebellion of her bastard half-brother Lord James Stewart, as well as during the coup attempt around the murder of her secretary Rizzio. Bothwell was thirty-two, and had just married, for her money, the heiress Jean Gordon. Mary was twenty-three, married to good-looking, empty-headed, self-important and stupid Lord Darnley (Bothwell would be implicated in his murder the following year). When Mary heard of Bothwell's injuries, she happened to be at Jedburgh, 25 miles away over the hills.

Whatever her merits as a monarch, Mary Queen of Scots was a talented hill traveller. She rode from Jedburgh to Hermitage Castle by hill paths to visit her wounded supporter. Later the same day she rode back again. Mary's pony trek to the bedside of the sexy scoundrel Bothwell made her even more unpopular than she already was with her Scots subjects, who were then engaged in converting themselves to Calvinism. According to John Knox, it was a love tryst. Today we'd quite like to believe this of romantic Mary. But Bothwell's wounds were severe, a September day is already short for the distance covered,

and Mary had several companions including her half-brother James Stewart (yes, he had just finished rebelling against her – but on the other hand he hadn't helped murder her secretary).

At the Queen's Mire on the descent from Cauldcleuch Head the Queen almost came to grief. According to Sir Walter Scott, it was still a place in his own time 'exhibiting, in many places, the bones of the horses which have been entangled in it'. More recent field drains have spoiled the historical ambiance.

The weather was so bad on the return journey that Mary fell dangerously ill. Later, during her long captivity in England, she wished: 'Would that I had died at Jedburgh.' After Mary's forced abdication, Bothwell fled to Denmark – John Prebble thinks it may actually have slipped his mind that he had a spurned former lover there: Anna Rustung. She captured him and he spent the last ten years of his life chained to a wall in a dungeon. Yes, the history is

ABOVE Old Gorrenberry, of fortified farmhouse or 'bastle' construction. The external stairs are the addition of a safer age; the living quarters originally would be reached by trapdoor from the livestock chamber below. According to Walter Scott, this house was endowed with a helpful brownie, performing household tasks at night in exchange for a saucer of milk. The gate sign shows that the brownie is still in service.

LEFT Newcastleton, known locally as Copshawholm. It's oddly orderly lines indicate a planned village, built to house weavers of wool, flax and cotton.

miserable. But the hill walk over Cauldcleuch Head, with grassy paths to the highest point hereabouts, is surprisingly enjoyable.

I didn't mention the second-wickedest holder of the castle. That accolade goes to Bothwell's nephew, Frances Stewart, Lord Bothwell. Reputedly involved in witchcraft himself, he will have appreciated the ghostly screams echoing around the night castle from victims of Lord Soulis. Bothwell the nephew launched not one but two daring raids aiming to kidnap the young King James VI (one against Holyroodhouse in Edinburgh, the second against Falkland Palace in Fife). Banished from Scotland, he established himself in Hermitage, raiding against England. He even played football in Eskdale in a match that was apparently 'declairit traitours' vs James's men. (Bothwell was fouled by the Master of Marishal: the final score is not recorded.)

After the Union of the Crowns, Bothwell ended his life as a cheap conjuror and fortune-teller in Naples. Meanwhile, with the Border lawlessness coming to its end, James VI sent the Governor of Berwick to cast down all the Liddesdale pele towers and castles. The place became the quiet side valley it still is. In 1792, government surveyors found no road at all, and no bridges. A few years later, Sir Walter Scott came ballad-hunting, and caused astonishment by arriving in a gig, the first wheeled vehicle ever seen in Liddesdale.

Newcastleton is an oddly orderly small settlement in this wild valley, built in 1793 by the 3rd Duke of Buccleuch as a weaving village. It was still brand new when Scott stayed in it, and found that, Elliots, Armstrongs and all, Christianity had still not entirely established itself. In the middle of family prayers, his host heard a rattling in the street and leapt from his knees: 'By Crivvens, here's the keg at last!' The illicit whisky, specially ordered in honour of Sir Walter, had arrived.

Half a century later, Liddesdale was transformed by the laying of the Waverley Line. This was an adventurous attempt by the North British Railway to compete with the Caledonian Railway's more natural route up the west coast. By the time it reached the Liddel, the daily Thames-Forth Express out of St Pancras had already passed along the equally wild and unlikely Settle–Carlisle Line, in a railway journey of free-enterprise optimism, implausible economics, and outstanding scenery.

Hermitage Water, evening.

From Newcastleton the trains ran up Liddesdale at 1:80, slowing to 30mph by top at Whitrope Tunnel. The following descent into Hawick was at the same steep gradient for 12 miles. The line skirted the Eildons, to pass above Melrose Abbey. Crossing the Tweed, those on the nightly sleeper service might catch a glimpse, as they took their breakfast, of Walter Scott's mansion at Abbotsford. After the thirteen bridges over Gala Water, there were the steep-sided Lammermuirs to cross.

The line was never economic and closed in 1969. Liddesdale could still summon up some lawlessness. The last train found the level crossing gates at Newcastleton locked against it. The local minister was arrested but released without charge.

Ettrick and Yarrow

The Scottish West March had a simple layout. In the west, Nithsdale and Annandale run down to the Solway; parallel with them, Eskdale runs south to the Debateable Land. And now in the Middle March, Liddesdale runs to the east of Eskdale before joining it at Johnie Armstrong's Gilnockie Tower.

And the next parallel valley, running south to the Border, is . . .

Well, it isn't. Look closely, and Liddesdale runs up more north-east than north. Inland from Gretna, the Border runs more north-east than east. And so Liddel actually runs parallel with the Border, never more than 5 miles down from the edge of England. And on the northern side of Liddesdale, over the moorland at the head of the Esk, three more glens run one behind the other, like troughs between high, green waves of the sea. While Liddesdale drains south-west to the Solway, the parallel Teviot, Ettrick and Yarrow glens behind it run north-east into the widening strath of the Tweed. And beyond Yarrow, over a last and largest hill ridge, lie the Tweed itself and Peebles.

From Liddesdale, then, the raiding routes run west across to the Esk. They run south to the Debateable Land, the Bewcastle Waste and the English West March. The head of Liddel turns east to Deadwater and the head of Tynedale in the English Middle March. Northwards again, high passes lead down to Hawick at the south-western corner of the Tweed's wide plain.

Meanwhile from Langholm and the Esk, the easy pass at Mosspaul carries the A7 through to Teviot, and again down to Hawick. From Teviot, head north across the rough moorland – or rather, today, struggle through the grim trees of Craik Forest – to the lovely twin glens of Ettrick and Yarrow. From the head of Yarrow, the A708, in the Southern Upland's loveliest through route, runs gently below the Grey Mare's Tail waterfall and along Moffat Water to blend into Annandale. From Ettrick Head a wild hill slot, one of the finest miles of the otherwise substandard Southern Upland Way, passes below Craigmichen Scar where the pioneering geologist Charles Lapworth once chipped out graptolites, before plunging through the plantations to Beattock on the Annan.

To see how this more-than-complex hill layout works in the hard practice of cattle raiding, examine the career of Auld Wat of Harden,

LEFT Ettrick Head, Capel Fell and Selcoth Burn. The old path now carrying the Southern Upland Way from Annandale to Ettrick runs across the steep slope on the right-hand side of the burn.

BELOW Ward Law, looking down to Ettrick Water, with Eildon Hills in the far distance.

on the lower Ettrick Water. His family motto was 'Cornua Reparabit Phoebe' – the horns of Phoebe will grow again, there's always another full moon. In 1592, he was with Bothwell of Hermitage on the daring raid to Falkland Palace in Fife, aiming to kidnap King James VI. In the summer of 1595, he pilfered a couple of horses from Geltsdale by Brampton in the English West March, followed by a 400-rider raid into Gilsland on the Roman Wall. The following year he was at Carlisle, second-in-command on the raid to rescue Kinmont Willie.

In 1597 his main target was Bellingham on the North Tyne, in the heart of the English Middle March. He killed three men and came home with 400 head of cattle. Returning from one of these rides, he passed a fine stack of hay, and told it: 'Aye, if ye had fower legs, ye wouldna stand there lang.'

Traced against the glens and hill ridges, all this makes – no sense at all. The reiving times had not only their own morality, but also, it seems, their own geography as well . . .

Some enlightenment comes from the Statistical Account of 1792. Even two centuries after Auld Wat, Ettrick had no bridges and only one road. And that road was 'so deep as greatly to obstruct travelling. The distance [to Selkirk] is about 16 miles, and it requires four hours to ride it. The snow, also, is a great inconvenience, often for many months.'

Ettrick to Gilsland is 40 miles as the crow flies. Auld Wat could do that in a night, by the hill paths – provided he didn't get bogged down crossing any valleys. One or two of those hill paths have been upgraded to roads today: roads of bare moorland, and sudden dips into cleuchs where the snow drifts deep, and hill edges where caravan-towers, innocently following their Satnav, wonder how long it would be before anyone spotted them upside down in the burn so far below. Mostly though, the old roads have faded to tracks of green grass, occasionally muddied up by the shepherd's quad bike, but the best of walking until they vanish into a bog created as a by-product of some modern hill drainage scheme.

Ettrickhall by road to the two lochs of Yarrow and Tibbie Shiels is 17 miles (if you're a caravan, though, go the extra 15 miles via Selkirk). But over the hill path it's just 5 miles. And so James Hogg, the poet known as the 'Ettrick Shepherd', would walk north over the hills to Tibbie Shiels Inn to meet up with Walter Scott. The shepherd's path, now part of the Southern Upland Way, runs

> Where the pools are bright and deep
> Where the grey trout lies asleep
> Up the river and o'er the lea
> That's the way for Billie and me.
> James Hogg: *A Boy's Song*

James Hogg looks across Yarrow to Tibbie Shiels Inn, beautifully sited between St Mary's Loch and the Loch of the Lowes. Tibbie had been a serving girl to Hogg's mother and, according to rumour, an early lover of James himself. She later nursed him in his final illness.

James Hogg, whose large marble statue broods over St Mary's Loch, was born in 1770 in the two-roomed clay cottage of Ettrickhall. He was also born into the oral tradition of folk tales. Hogg's mother Margaret Laidlaw was a story teller, especially of ghost stories. His grandfather, William Laidlaw of Over Phawhope, was an illicit distiller and the last man in the Borders to talk to the fairies. Laidlaw would claim (to the credulous) that at his birth, with the Ettrick in flood, the midwife was carried across to him by the loyal household brownie (the kind of servile spirit referred to as 'house-elf' as in the Harry Potter opus).

Aged seven, Hogg was at work as that lowest form of rural life, a herd-boy at Craigyrigg on the Yarrow. A ewe lamb and a pair of shoes were his half year's wage. Aged fourteen, he saved up to buy a violin, and his practising in the barn was more than once taken for the screechings of demons. He was composing in two unrelated styles: vernacular and rather rude songs to play on his fiddle; and stultified imitations of the classical verse of Pope and Dryden. His surprising ambition to become a literary poet was in no way based on the example of Burns. Of Burns he had never heard, until he was hit like a bombshell by 'Tam o' Shanter', not read from any book but recited to him by a half-daft travelling laddie.

By 1802 Hogg was combining the tough life of a Border shepherd with day trips to the Edinburgh literary scene. He soon found that, while a twelvemonth of hard labour on a hill farm earned him a net loss of 20 guineas, he could earn a quarter of that in profit with a single poem.

> Her bonny breast, sae fair and dink,
> Nae man may safely ponder on;
> But ye may sigh, and ye may think
> Of rosebud on an ivory cone;

Or cream-curd frae the silver cup,
Sae gelid an' sae round to see,
An' plantit on its yielding top
A ripe red little strawberry.

This closely observed tribute to his future wife, Margaret Phillips from Nithsdale, earned him that five guineas. Clearly the *Scots Magazine* was a racier publication in 1812 than it is today.

The unsettling *Confessions of a Justified Sinner* was published in 1825. It never made a profit for its author or its publisher, and was ignored for the next 100 years, after which, 'I read it with a stupefaction and admiration which increased with every page,' wrote the French novelist André Gide. Hogg also contributed 'Battle of Otterburn' and at least two other ballads, passed down from his mother, to Scott's *Border Minstrelsey*.

Here's a story from Hogg's mother about their own ancestor witch, and how she got the better of a famous neighbour, the sorcerer Michael Scott of Aikwood Tower.

Michael Scott took his dogs out, pretending to go hunting. But he was really going to the Witch of Fauldshope to see if she was any good. 'Show us a spell, witch,' he pestered, until she struck him three times with her wand and turned him into a hare.

'Shoo, Michael, rin or dee!' She set his own dogs on him, and they chased him all the way home. He escaped by crawling in through the sewer pipe.

In reprisal, Scott left a spell over the witch's doorway. Everyone who passed into her house took off all their clothes and was seized by a dancing mania. Once the magic note was discovered and burnt, they returned to their senses and put their clothes back on. But by that time it was too late for the witch, who had danced herself to death.

Another story concerned the Witch of Kirkhope, further down the valley. Some gentlemen came to hunt the King's forest of Ettrick. They weren't getting anywhere until a lad offered to improve the sport for a fee of a guinea. There was a condition: the lad was to keep hold of one dog, the black greyhound. They must have been proper gents because they agreed the rather large fee (in 1750, a guinea was about £150 in today's money). At once, a hare started up in front of the dogs, and led them a chase up and down the glen.

One of the gents (maybe not such a gentleman after all) sneaked up behind the lad, and cut the lead of the black greyhound. And the lad cried out: 'Run, Mither, run! If ever ye ran in your life!'

The black dog got closer … and closer … It was just reaching for the hare when it leapt through the Kirkhope cottage window, just west of Ettrickbridge (grid reference NT380237). Inside the house, they found no hare, but an old woman lying on the bed, panting so hard she couldn't speak a word.

But what of the black hound? I have my own idea. As a witch's son the lad was equipped with a bridle ring made of iron. Looking through it, he'd have recognised the black greyhound as none other than Michael Scott himself, out for a day's fun from his tower 4 miles down the glen.

As I walked St Cuthbert's Way long-distance path near Morebattle, a hare sat in the road ahead, looking back. Every time I got close it loped on ahead, then sat up and looked at me again. Was it some spirit guide? Probably not. Hares just do that. Their safety depends on knowing what's going on, and they're fast enough that they can take time to look things over before running away. And then, when the hares turn white with the first snow, yes, it is magical. So while foxes and crows are usually just foxes and crows, it's no surprise when hares turn out to be witches in disguise.

Dryhope Tower, at the foot of St Mary's Loch.

PEEBLES AND THE TWEED

From Peebles to the edge of England you must cross the Manor Hills, Yarrow Water, Ettrick Water, Teviot and Liddesdale. Peebles is now a commuter suburb of Edinburgh. Its tough salmon-referencing motto *Incrementum Contranatando* (I increase by swimming against the flow) is being modernised to the banal 'Peebles for Pleasure'.

So why is Peebles part of the Border land?

Well, it's in today's Borders Region. More than that, it's the start-point of old reiving paths across the Manor Hills to Talla and the Devil's Beeftub, and south-east into Yarrow and Ettrick – one of them is still named on maps as the Thieves' Road. And finally, Peebles is Border because of its fine Border castle at Neidpath, once besieged by Oliver Cromwell. Then there's Barns Tower, just 2 miles upstream. Don't let the pink paintwork deceive you; this is an authentic Border pele.

BELOW Pink pele at Barns Tower, up the Tweed from Peebles.

RIGHT ABOVE Peebles and the Tweed, from Cademuir Hill.

RIGHT MIDDLE Manor Hills: Glenshiels Banks to Dun Rig, above Traquair.

RIGHT BELOW Hundleshope farm at the edge of the Manor Hills, seen from Cademuir.

Outlook from Eildon

If thou would'st view fair Melrose aright,
Go visit it by the pale moonlight . . .
When the broken arches are black in night,
And each shafted oriel glimmers white

Walter Scott: *Lay of the Last Minstrel*

The triple hill of Eildon rises above Melrose at what is, by strict geography, the northern edge of the Border country. The Border itself is, at its closest point, 25 miles away. That closest point is, surprisingly, to the east and slightly north of Eildon, down the Tweed at Carham where the Border runs north to the river.

Southwards from Eildon, though, the Border is almost as close. Away beyond Jedburgh, the skyline dips at the pass of Carter Bar, just 30 miles away. South-eastwards, the line shrugs upwards to the dome of the Cheviot, 40 miles away. Just west of south rises Cauldcleuch Head, high point of Roxburghshire above Hermitage Castle. And looking away to the west, White Coomb and the steep hills around Ettrick Head are only slightly further. The Eildons blip into the northward view from hills of more than half the borderline.

Eildon rises only 1,000 feet above the wide strath of the Tweed. But it is made of tough volcanic basalt, the remnants of a big intrusion within the old red sandstones of Tweeddale, so Eildon's thousand feet are steep ones. You look down on to Melrose and trace the curves of the Tweed.

Eildon is a viewpoint outwards over the geography, but even more: back through time. Over in those hills of Ettrick and Yarrow this book has visited the Border reivers, and they'll be at it again, burning and murdering in the English valleys beyond the Cheviot. But the Border is more, both before and also after the reiving times. And Eildon is the place to survey it all.

Immediately below the second summit, Eildon Hill North, a plateau shows the walls of an Iron Age settlement. There are almost a hundred hut circles hidden in the heather of the summit itself. The small but pointy foothills on the Scottish side of Cheviot were, it seems, prime housing locations 2,000 years ago. Almost every hilltop there has its earthwork, a green ring around a large green fingertip.

Eildon's steep rise was just as attractive to the Romans, and a natural waymark for the surveyors who laid Dere Street across the high ridge of the Cheviot. They called their large fort *Trimontium*, or triple-hill. It's vanished now under the suburban brickwork of Newstead. But Dere Street itself can be traced as you look from Eildon's top. It lies under the A68, then is marked by a ruler-straight line of field edges towards the distant green-brown hills.

The Eildon Hills rise 300m above the Tweed basin, to see and be seen along 40 miles of the Border. On the plateau at bottom left, part of an Iron Age settlement can be made out.

A lad called Cuthbert ran sheep over those hills. After a vision of St Aidan on a sleepy afternoon, Cuthbert came to Old Melrose, an abbey now vanished in the loop of Tweed below Eildon's eastern spur. Monks from Melrose used the Roman ways through the hills on their long-distance hikes across Britain, linking Iona in the Hebrides with Lindisfarne on the Northumberland coast. Cuthbert's own journey would take him to Lindisfarne, as abbot and then bishop.

In the present century, a long-distance path (at 100 kilometres, it's quite a short long-distance path) traces Cuthbert's life journey. From Melrose it crosses between two peaks of Eildon, follows Roman Dere Street, and ranges the Cheviot foothills to Wooler. There's no better way of making the acquaintance of the eastern borderland, while injecting a small amount of cash into the economy of Teviot and Glendale.

Cuthbert's Way starts at the replacement Melrose Abbey, built as recently as 1136 and still mostly standing. Binoculars would reveal other abbey ruins at Dryburgh by St Boswells, at Jedburgh, and away in the east, at Kelso. Another long-distance path links the four, the 64-mile Border Abbeys Way. Any monastery along the Border tended to get destroyed and rebuilt from time to time.

The final knockdown came in the English campaign of 1544 called the Rough Wooing. Henry VIII decided to solve his Scottish problem by marrying off Mary Queen of Scots, at the time just months old, to his infant son Edward. When the Scots declined to become England's daughter-in-law, Henry sent the Earl of Hertford to persuade them. The raid extended far into Scotland: Edinburgh was sacked and Dumfries destroyed.

In Teviotdale alone, the English – assisted by enthusiastic Borderers including Nixons, Crosers, Olivers and Rutherfords – destroyed seven monasteries, sixteen castles and pele towers, five market towns and 243 villages. Particular attention was paid to the defensive infrastructure of bastles, small shelters for individual households against neighbourly raids, and almost none of these was left standing on the Scottish side.

In February 1545 a small Scots army caught up with Hertford at Ancrum Moor, just down the Roman Road from Eildon. The English, used to easy victories, scarcely believed they were being attacked. But the Scots had placed themselves with the sun at their backs and also the wind, and fired the heather in the Englishmen's faces. Charging hopefully through the smoke, the English knights impaled themselves on the shiltrom, or hedge of spears. At which point the Nixons and Crosers realised that they had, most atypically, attached themselves to the losing side. Tearing off the crosses of St George from their chests, they attacked the English from behind. Even the locals joined in, including an angry lass called Lilliard.

> Upon the English loons
> She laid many thumps
> And when her legs were cuttit off
> She fought upon her stumps.
> [loons = lads]

It's a shame to spoil a story by excessive research. So ignore that the place was named Lilliard's Cross even before the battle happened. The rhyme of 'laid many thumps' with 'fought upon stumps' also predates Ancrum Moor, having occurred in the 'Ballad of Chevy Chase', a battle in the English Middle March 150 years before. It is, in fact, a leg-end legend.

Having cast the historic Eildon eye northwards at Melrose, south to the Roman road and Ancrum Moor, and at the reivers' hill country all around, one direction is still unexplored: directly downwards. Inside Eildon Hill

BELOW LEFT Melrose Abbey. St Cuthbert's one was two miles away in a loop of the Tweed. But this one has the buried heart of Robert the Bruce, impish gargoyles, and a small museum of Roman antiquities.

BELOW Archway ornament, Melrose Abbey.

lives, or used to live, the Queen of the Fairies. Some time in the thirteenth century, Thomas the Rhymer of Ercildoune (Earlston, 4 miles north of Melrose) lay down for a nap above the abbey.

> True Thomas lay on Huntlie bank
> Spying ferlies wi' his ee;
> And there he saw a lady bright
> come riding down by the Eildon Tree.
> [ferlie = marvel]

It was Shakespeare in *A Midsummer Night's Dream* who reinvented fairies as cute little creatures dancing in the bowl of a buttercup. The Victorians developed this into an excuse for dressing young ladies up in a few rose petals and taking photographs of them. The true fairies were not actually evil, but they were capricious and powerful, and to be avoided on the whole. Their gifts of gold tended to turn to thistledown, and their idea of fun was having you dance all night and the next night and for seven years until the feet wore off the ends of your legs.

Thomas must have been both lucky and clever to have kept their Queen in a friendly mood. Seven years later, he emerged again from Eildon with the gift of prophesy. And in 1929 the Melrose Literary Society raised a marker stone at the site of the Eildon Tree as a warning to all of us to take our snooze somewhere else.

RIGHT The large Iron Age settlement on Eildon hill was the tribal capital of the Selgovae, but it's hard to make it out under the heather. The grassy Cheviots make it all more obvious. An Iron Age wall rings the top of Yeavering Bell, west of Wooler.

BELOW Between the Roman Wall and the Forth–Clyde valley, the Romans never fully settled the Southern Uplands, but they did build a shifting network of roads and forts. This is Chew Green, where Dere Street crosses the Cheviots.

It was in about 1750 that the fairies departed from the Border country. Patie Oliver of the Jed Water saw the last fairy leaving the Brocklaw, above Hyndlee farm. (Hundale is opposite Ferniehurst Castle, 2 miles south of Jedburgh. The hill is called Black Law on Landranger maps.)

A wee little creature a' clad in green, an' wi' lang hair, yellow as gowd, hingin' round its shoulders, whiles gi'en a whink o' a greet, an' aye atween its haunds raisin' a queer, unyirthly cry, 'Hae ye seen Hewie Milburn? Oh! Hae ye seen Hewie Milburn?' The creature was no bigger than a three-year-auld lassie, but feat and ticht, lithe o' limb as any grown woman, an' its face was the doonright perfection o' beauty, only there was something wild and unyirthly in its e'en that couldna be lookit at: it aye taigl't on aboot the bucht, repeatin' its cry, 'Hae ye seen Hewie Milburn?'

Were the green hills of the Borders congenial to the fairy folk? Or was it that the fairy stories here were passed down just long enough to be collected by Walter Scott? Scott, who is himself the final ferlie (or marvel) seen by the eye of history from Eildon Hill – his main mansion of Abbotsford lies just two miles away up the Tweed.

Walter Scott

Walter Scott was born in 1771, the son of an Edinburgh solicitor. He was lame from polio, and, for the sake of strengthening him up, he was sent to his grandparents' farm. This happened to be in the shadow of Smailholm, one of the finest of the Border peles. One day the little fellow went missing in a thunderstorm. They found him 'lying in the grass at the foot of the old grey strength, clapping his hands at each flash and shouting: "Bonny! Bonny!"'

He was schooled briefly in Kelso at his aunt Jenny's, but mainly in Edinburgh. Aged fifteen, he was briefly in the same salon with Robert Burns. 'Who wrote the poem that goes with this print?' Burns asked. Young Walter was the one who knew the answer. Aged twenty, we see him at Langleeford under the Cheviot with his uncle, and already in a letter to a friend he is enthusiastic about the Borders and their stories.

Behold a letter from the mountains, in one of the wildest and most romantic situations, which your imagination, fertile upon the subject of cottages, ever suggested. To add to my satisfaction we are amidst places renowned by feats of former days; each hill is crowned with a tower, or camp, or cairn; and in no situation can you be near more fields of battle — Flodden, Otterburn, and Chevy Chase. Ford Castle, Chillingham Castle, Coupland Castle and many another scene of blood are within the compass of a forenoon's ride. . . . My uncle drinks the whey here [goatsmilk whey, for its health-giving properties], as I do ever since I understood it was brought to his bedside every morning at six, by a very pretty dairymaid. So much simplicity resides amongst those hills that a pen, which could write at least, was not to be found about the house, though belonging to a considerable farmer, till I shot the crow with whose quill I write this epistle.

In 1796, Scott's first publication was the *Minstrelsy of the Scottish Border* – his compilation of the traditional stories and ballads. One of them features his own ancestor, the brutal Border raider Auld Wat of Harden. *Minstrelsy* also shows Scott's habit of tampering with the texts. We shall never know what over-explicit phrase the original ballad used for the Captain of Bewcastle's upper leg injury.

Smailholm Tower stands on a handy outcrop of tough dolerite midway between Kelso and Melrose.

In 1799 Scott was appointed sheriff-depute of Selkirk, and moved from Edinburgh to the Tweed. In 1805 came the long poem 'The Lay of the Last Minstrel'. It's a love story in ballad style, set against the background of the Kerr/Scott feuds of Teviotdale. 'The inhabitants living in a state partly pastoral and partly warlike, and combining habits of constant depredation with the influence of a rude spirit of chivalry, were often engaged in scenes highly susceptible of poetical ornament.'

In 1814 his first novel, *Waverley*, was published without his name on, as he considered himself a poet and the book a discreditable pot boiler. In 1820 he was honoured as a baronet, and in 1822 orchestrated the visit to Scotland of King George IV. Scottishness, as we know it today – knife in the sock, bagpipes and boxes of shortbread with a wee tartan ribbon – it was all invented by Sir Walter in 1820. Since the dawn of history, the English have been wondering what the Scotsman wears underneath the kilt. In 1822, for the first time and under King George's one, the answer was flesh coloured tights.

In the 1820s, writers could earn serious money. Scott bought a Tweedside cottage with the unpromising name of Clartyhole (clarty means mucky or boggy). Over seven years and at a cost of £25,000 (about £500,000 in today's terms) he transformed it into a romantic mansion. John Ruskin judged Abbotsford 'perhaps the most incongruous pile that gentlemanly modernism ever designed'. It contains a large leather-bound library and an awful lot of armour.

In 1825 came a crisis in the banking system, which had become dependent on lucrative but dodgy investments, notably in South America. The 'sub-prime' dealings including a country called Poyais which turned out to be the invention of an enterprising Scotsman called Gregor Macgregor. Nearly seventy UK banks failed, and the stock market collapsed. The system of letters of credit left Scott personally liable for his printers' debts of £102,000 – around £20 million today. Sir Walter considered it dishonourable to declare bankruptcy, and set himself to write his way out of debt.

In 1832, exhausted by the non-stop writing of the twenty-six Waverley novels, he died. The Waverley Novels went on selling, and eventually paid off the whole of the debt.

Scott may have invented the historical novel, but his own ones soon attracted mockery. The oath 'Great Scott!' derives from a spoof by Mark Twain in *A Connecticut Yankee in the Court of King Arthur* (1889). Scott's chivalrous heroes are tiresome, but his 'spunky lass' heroines can be quite fun while many of his minor characters are a delight. And 'Young Lochinvar' is a rattling piece of rhyme.

Jedburgh main street, decorated for its annual Callant's Festival or march-riding, which commemorates the town's part in the Redeswire Raid of 1575 (see pages 67–8). Jedburgh was as fierce as any small town of the Borders, and was for many years at feud with the Kerrs of nearby Ferniehurst Castle. The town has its own weapon, the 2-metre-long Jeddart axe; its own feared war cry of 'Jeddart's Here!'; and its own legal system, 'Jeddart justice', which consisted of hanging the accused straight away and proceeding to trial at some later date. Jethart Snails are however harmless, being a boiled sweet introduced by prisoners from the Napoleonic Wars.

ABOVE Hawick and its town hall of 1886. Despite losing its status as the 'Glasgow of the South', Hawick remains a vigorous wee town, especially during the yearly Common Riding with its weird war-cry: 'Teribus ye teri odin'. That event commemorates an event of 1514, the year after the Battle of Flodden. A party under the Prior of Hexham's steward came north to take advantage of the way most of the menfolk had been killed in that battle. Relaxing by the Teviot after their pillage of nearby Denholm, they were surprised and killed by the fatherless lads (the 'callants') of Hawick.

LEFT Old Wilton Mills, Hawick. In the 1870s, 500 tons of knitted goods were being produced each year. Andrew Lang, in 1911, described the water of the Teviot as 'varying, when last I shuddered at it, from black to a most unwholesome light blue.' In 1972 Nigel Tranter wrote that 'in every corner of the world where top quality knitwear is esteemed, Hawick and the names of its famous jumpers, sweaters, cardigans are household words'. Today, Hawick's river is clean, its woollen industry extinct.

TOP Denholm village, at the foot of Rubers Law.

ABOVE Haining Loch, part of the town park of Selkirk. The trees above the lake grow out of a Norman motte and bailey. Selkirk lies at the entrance of Ettrick and Yarrow. During the Wars of Independence these formed a wild and wooded refuge against the English, and William Wallace's short-lived parliament was established at Selkirk. Being a little further in from the Border, it was burned less frequently than Hawick and Jedburgh. Even so, it still got it after Flodden. Of eighty volunteers to the battle just one man returned, but with a captured English flag. The town's march-riding commemorates this.

Dark Ruberslaw, that lifts his head sublime,
Rugged and hoary with the wrecks of time;
On his broad misty front the giant wears
The horrid furrows of ten thousand years.

John Leyden of Denholm, born in 1775, was another of the
Borders' 'lads o' pairts' or peasant prodigies. He became
fluent in eight languages including his own, wrote a three-
volume history of African exploration, edited the *Scots
Magazine*, and was appointed a judge in Calcutta, before dying
in Java aged thirty-six. He was also a ballad-gatherer for Walter
Scott, who tells how Leyden walked 40 miles to get the last
two verses of a ballad and returned at midnight, singing it all
the way with his loud, harsh voice. The ballad on Kielder Stane
later in this book was collected and then improved by Leyden.

ABOVE Roxburgh Castle, in the angle where Teviot meets Tweed, guarded the Tweed's lowest ford above Berwick. Roxburgh, 'Rex Burgh', was founded by David I (reigned 1124–53) as his capital. Being too close to England, it was destroyed at various times in Wars of Independence. From 1306 to 1310 Robert the Bruce's captured sister Mary was suspended from the castle walls in an iron cage. In 1460, James II was besieging the castle, then held by the English. He was admiring the tremendous effect of his own great brass bombast called 'The Lion', when it exploded and killed him. The castle and its burgh were then overrun and destroyed by grief-stricken Scots under command of the newly widowed Queen Mary.

LEFT James II as seen at Dryburgh Abbey, with (above his head) one of the cannon that killed him. Of Scotland's six Jameses, only the final one (James I of England) reached old age.

Floors Castle, seen from the ruins of Roxburgh Castle. It is Fleurs on old maps. The original building was the current central block in moderately ornamented form. Under the influence of Sir Walter Scott, the 6th Earl of Roxburgh commissioned improvements by the fashionable Edinburgh architect W.H. Playfair. Floors is the largest inhabited house in Scotland, and was Greystoke, the ape-man's ancestral childhood home, in the early Tarzan films.

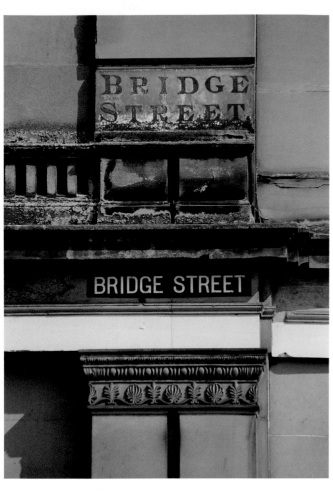

OPPOSITE AND LEFT Kelso burgh grew around its abbey, founded by David I as a civilising and improving measure, with Tironensian (craftsman and useful skills type) monks. The town had a mill and two ferries across the Tweed. An attempt to sterilize houses of plague victims resulted in the town being burned down in 1645, and it burned again, to the ground this time, in 1684. The town was then rebuilt from a public subscription across all Scotland, to give the present planned and handsome Georgian town centre.

BELOW Cessford Castle, refuge of Robert Kerr, Scottish Middle March Warden. From here he conducted his feud with English Warden Robert Cary (see Chapter 8). Observers at the time weren't sure if Kerr was the most vicious and effective of the Border warlords: the Bold Buccleuch of Teviotdale was perhaps even worse. In 1600, with Border feuding coming to its end, Kerr became the first Earl of Roxburghe. Within a century his heirs were constructing Floors Castle.

5 CHEVIOT HILLS

The English seized the Cheviot and its foothills in 1154. The annexation was placed on a formal footing in 1174 by the Treaty of Falaise. But that treaty was signed under duress: William the Lion (of Scotland) was a prisoner in the Tower of London at the time. Anyway, it was superseded in 1189, when Richard the Lionheart sold southern Scotland back to Scotland (as it were) for 10,000 merks to finance the Third Crusade. Some time in the autumn of 1999, as Scottish devolution was being decided in a haze of pipe smoke in a back room off the Royal Mile, men in climbing boots, kilts and beards must surely have convened to consider the status of these lost hills.

In the case of the Cheviot itself, it might be friendly to let the English keep the thing. The approach to Cheviot from Wooler is up the so-called 'permissive path'. The only permissive activity you can imagine here is mud wrestling. The dismal path plods up through the mist into the summit slurry. Here the black sloppy stuff is knee deep. Will it eventually be trampled neck-deep, making the Cheviot an impregnable summit ringed by forlorn peaty peak-baggers? Or will the ooze trickle down the sides, to expose a compacted under-surface of lost footwear, orange peel and peat-preserved wrinkled hill walkers? Already two trig points have sunk; the third stands on a raft of breeze-blocks still trying to keep its head above the mud.

The Northumberland National Park's rangers have laid a line of yellow sandstone slabs across the plateau. Some have objected to these, as they tame the natural rigours of the bog. As far as I am concerned, they can pave over the entire hill, and the sooner the better. Then we can have a shopping mall up there, with tartan souvenirs, Costa Coffee and outdoor shops.

Any reconquest of the Cheviot would require an amendment to Corbett's Tables. This is the list of Scottish hills lower than Munros but over 2,500 feet (762m) high, published by the Scottish Mountaineering Club. The list includes Merrick in the Galloway Hills, Goatfell on Arran, Beinn Dearg of Torridon, and the Cobbler in Arrochar. The northernmost Corbett is Ben Loyal, an eagle-haunted crag looking across at the Orkney Isles. Allow a mud pie like the Cheviot onto the southern end and Ben Loyal might depart in disgust and paddle out across the North Sea to relocate as a mountain of Norway.

In a fine display of not letting logic stand in the way of a good idea, the 1984 edition of the Tables dealt with the Cheviot in both of two possible ways. In the list of Corbetts the Cheviot did not appear. In the list of Donalds (Scottish hills over 2,000 feet in the Southern Uplands), the Cheviot did

LEFT The Cheviot seen across the Teviot plains. Daniel Defoe climbed it in 1726: 'One "Pico or Master-Hill" higher than all the rest by a great deal, which, at a distance, looks like the Pico-Teneriffe at the Canaries, and is so high, that I remember it is seen plainly from the Rosemary-Top in the East Riding of Yorkshire.' As if the comparison with Mount Teide (3,718m) isn't absurd enough, James Logan Mack got overexcited by a winter view from inside the Hen Hole: 'Without doubt, before me was a perfect miniature of the Jungfrau as seen from Interlaken, and every whit as impressive.' Roseberry Topping, 81 miles away on the North York Moors, is indeed visible from the Cheviot, as is Scafell Pike at the same distance and Lochnagar at 111 miles.

ABOVE Defoe's 'Pico-Teneriffe', Mount Teide. Quite like the Cheviot?

ABOVE RIGHT Summit of the Cheviot.

appear, together with eight of its foothills. Five of those foothills are also in present-day England, the other three on the Union Boundary.

In the 1997 edition of the Tables the Scottish Mountaineering Club rather naughtily pre-empted the Scottish Assembly and dropped the six English hills. Presumably they were not expecting any reconquest before the next re-issue of the Tables, or possibly the editor had traversed the 10-mile borderline range between Deadwater Fell and Carter Bar. It's a watershed that fails to shed any water: a wide, flat place of peat and heather where the most interesting moment is a decaying fence post.

At this point it's traditional to evoke the mind-expanding emptiness of the Border hills. The wind rattling the heather stalks, the hollow tinkle of water into a peat hole, the yellow-brown, rounded hills range beyond range, fading into the grey of a raincloud. The delicious solitude is of course caused by the hillwalkers all having cleared off somewhere nice, like the Lake District.

Ecologically speaking, what we walk on is not even the original condition of this hill country. It used to be far, far worse. Subsidised hill drainage schemes have tamed what used to be lethal. The 'Queen's Mire' on Cauldcleuch Head, where in Scott's day the white bones of horses still poked up out of the peat, is now an ordinary patch of uncomfortable tussocks. In better times, the Tarras Moss above Langholm, the mountain refuge of the Armstrongs, had bogs where two spears tied together couldn't reach the bottom.

Between those bogs were scrubby woodlands, and Robert Cary referred to the place as Tarras Wood: 'So surrounded with bogges and marish grounds, and thicke bushes and shrubbes, as they [the Armstrongs] feared not the force nor power of England nor Scotland, so long as they were there.' His hunt against them – in effect, a game of copse and robbers – is described in the chapter on the English Middle March. Walter Scott notes in 1796: 'There are now no trees in Liddesdale, except on the banks of the rivers, where they are protected from sheep. But the stumps and fallen timber, which are everywhere found in the morasses, attest how well the country must have been wooded in former days.'

One ballad, 'The Sang of the Outlaw Murray', describes the trees of the Tweed at Caddonfoot, north of Selkirk:

> The King was cuming thro' Caddon Ford,
> And full five thousand men was he;
> They saw the derke Foreste them before,
> They thought it awsome for to see.

At Carrifran above Moffatdale, volunteers and the John Muir Trust are recreating this awesome ancient woodland. Their birches, rowan, alder and oak scrub are now high enough to shut out the surroundings, though they are a long way from the fallen timber and black soggy bits, the low branches, the thigh-high bracken and bramble that must have made the wildwood as cursedly uncomfortable, whether on foot or on horse, as any modern plantation of Christmas trees. Albeit considerably richer in robins.

LEFT Trees, when you leave them to it. A few scraps of ancient woodland survive, and some has recently been replanted at Carrifran above Moffat Water. This waste ground beside the Tweed at St Boswells isn't ancient, but still shows why reivers preferred the high ways across the hills.

ABOVE The exact line of the Border across this remote stretch of tussocks, east of Chew Green, was only settled in 1838. It follows the stream in the middle distance. The foreground post marks the Pennine Way.

RIGHT The Street, an old drove road above Coquetdale.

Redeswire Raid

After 10 miles of the toughest and possibly least enjoyable hill ground anywhere in the UK, the Border walker emerges at Carter Bar. The grey roadway of the A68 rises out of England; it passes between the red cross of St George and the blue one of St Andrew; and drops northwards into Scotland. In a guidebook of 1926, the A6088 branch towards Hawick is described as 'partially grass grown'.

Four hundred years ago, on an agreed day of every month, an armed band would approach this point up out of Redesdale, and another one southwards from the headwaters of the Jed. After counting each other's lances, the Warden of the Scottish Middle March and his English counterpart would advance for a cautious handshake across the Border.

At the Warden meeting of 7 June 1575, the principals were Sir John Carmichael, Keeper of Liddesdale (and a good one, later murdered by the Armstrongs, technically on his own side) and Sir John Forster, English Middle March Warden (a ruffian even by March Warden standards). Forster had brought a small army up out of Redesdale and Tynedale, so the Scots were outnumbered – which, in theory, shouldn't have mattered at all.

> Some gaed to drink, and some stude still,
> And some to cards and dice them sped:
> Till on ane Farnstein they fyled a bill,
> And he was fugitive and fled.

As Farnstein was an Englishman with a complaint against him from the Scots, Forster should have brought him along. In the discussion of why he hadn't done so, Forster made some remarks about Carmichael's family. Catching the mood of the moment, the men of Redesdale and Tynedale let off a flight of arrows. The Scots were unprepared:

> But little harness [armour] had we there;
> But auld Badreule had on a jack,
> And did right weel, I you declare,
> With all his Turnbulls at his back.

Ditch marking the Border line on the Scottish slope of Lamb Hill. Today's Border follows the watershed fence just above.

Despite the efforts of my ancestor Sir Andrew Turnbull of Bedrule, the Scots had the worst of it, and Carmichael was made prisoner. But as the Tynedale men were getting stuck into looting the prisoners and the peddler's booths, the townsfolk of Jedburgh came up the hill to join in the fun.

> With help of God the game gaed right,
> Frae time the foremost of them fell;
> Then ower the knowe, without goodnight
> They ran with mony a shout and yell.

Sir George Heron of Chipchase, the English Deputy Warden, was killed, 'to the great regret of both parties', says Walter Scott, a sound Warden being valued on either side of the Border. Forster the English Warden and many of the English tribal leaders were captured and sent to Edinburgh. The King's Regent, the Earl of Morton, greeted them respectfully, even making them gifts of Scottish falcons – with the observation that they had a noble exchange, receiving live hawks for dead Herons. He kept them in the castle until everybody's tempers had cooled, and thus avoided what could have turned into the final all-out war between the two nations.

The way from Carter Bar to Windy Gyle is by grassy paths with hardly any bog and steep little valleys running away into Scotland. A Roman road runs across, made wide and comfortable by generations of drovers and cattle-thieves. Northwards are small pointy hills each with its own Iron Age hillfort. The views, especially into Scotland, are huge. And in the middle distance of every northward view poke up the three wee Eildons.

Walking northwards for Berwick, I passed this way on a sunny Saturday with people in bright jackets sprinkled along the ridge. It being the twenty-first century, I approached them without wondering if they might be inclined, either for profit or simple pleasure, to cut me down and leave my body for the crows. We discussed the weather, and if it was likely to rain (it wasn't), and left each other completely still alive.

Here the Pennine Way runs along the Border ridge and a wooden shelter hut stands on Lamb Hill. A note from the shepherd asked residents not to cross the Border fence in order to defecate on Scotland. This is not a political jibe but just because his dogs tend to roll in it.

From Windy Gyle to Cheviot is a slabbed path. It could be an urban pavement, with white flecks of cotton grass standing in for the urban litter of cigarette packets and crisp wrappers. The English have planted their side of it with spruce. The ground rises over many miles to Cheviot summit with its beige paving, black bog and fence posts collapsing into the squalid surface.

From hellhole to Hen Hole: I walked away from it all westwards until a deep grassy hollow opened below my toes. Down in the hollow were small waterfalls, wildflowers, and grey boulders gleaming from the recent rain. The way out was between slabby crags. The Hen Hole is a cavity of grey scree and bright grasses, big enough for several million hens or for a fair herd of stolen cattle. It's Northumberland's patch of mountain, and it's good.

South of here, Hedgehope has a nice name and a nice sea view. And then there are the little valleys – Coquetdale, Uswayburn, the Breamish. The valley sides are steep and high, sculpted in the austere school of Henry Moore or Bridget Riley, with touches of decorative levity supplied by the odd granite tor. Wind whispers in the yellow grasses, and a merry little stream runs out along the bottom.

Recapture the Cheviot? That's a tricky one. The Treaty of Falaise has not been recognised by the United Nations. On the other hand, it might be better to wait until it's time for a new edition of Munro's Tables.

The Southern Uplands are shales and sandstones, but the Cheviots are volcanic. This rhyolite on Windy Gyle is a lava, with gas-bubble holes.

ARE THE BORDERS BEAUTIFUL?

I viewed with mute surprise, I may almost say with disappointment, the mere succession of grey waving hills, line beyond line, as far as my eye could reach, monotonous in their aspect, and destitute of trees.

Washington Irving, *Abbotsford and Newstead Abbey* (1835)

On the other hand:

There is an attraction in these billowy uplands which increases the better we know them; beauty in the mighty stretches of green pasture sloping upwards and backwards, as often as not vanishing into grey mist in the acres of waving brake, the many-coloured rocks and boulders, the flashing streams and burns, the flowers and wild birds, less wild here than in the peopled lowlands. Then there is the silence and all-aloneness of the Borderlands.

John Cordeaux, ornithologist (1870s)

LEFT, ABOVE The Hanging Stone on the south-west slope of Cairn Hill marked the corner of the English Middle and East Marches. This view looks west over Scotland.

LEFT, BELOW Russell's Cairn, a Bronze Age pile of stones on the eastern slope of Windy Gyle. Like Redeswire Moor, this was a rendezvous point on days of truce. Breaking of the truce-day was the exception rather than the rule; so when Lord Francis Russell, who had already survived the Redeswire Fray, was shot dead in 1585, this large cairn was renamed in commemoration. (Maps wrongly mark as Russell's Cairn the one on Windy Gyle summit, half a mile to the east.)

RIGHT The Cheviots at daybreak from Hownam Law. The Cheviot is on the right, with the Border Ridge running down the skyline.

BELOW Where Cheviots are concerned, small is shapely, especially on the Scottish side. Hownam Law has a large Iron Age hillfort.

LEFT Hadrian's Wall passes westwards into Cumbria through the Gilsland Gap, which gives easy access from the English West March to Haltwhistle and the Tyne. Thirlwall Castle, at Greenhead, sits in the gap. Its name means 'gap in the wall', and the Roman wall supplied its building stones.

BELOW The bastle, or defensible farmhouse, built in the south entrance of Housesteads Roman fort on Hadrian's Wall. Beds of limestone and gritstone give the landscape below a horizontal layered look. The small Grindon Lough lies on one of the waterproof gritstone layers.

6 ENGLISH MIDDLE MARCH

Haltwhistle and the Wall

North of the Cheviots, streams run down to the wide hinterland of the Teviot and Tweed. Southwards, a similar hinterland is the Tyne Gap from Haltwhistle to Hexham, the band of low country traversed by Hadrian's Wall.

The Tyne however runs due east, while the Cheviot ridge and the borderline along it slant away north-east. At its western end, the South Tyne

runs close to the corner of Bewcastle Waste, and its corner at Haltwhistle is just 18 miles of rough riding from the Kershope fords at the start of Scotland.

But downstream, as the Border withdraws north, the land between Hadrian's Wall and the Border becomes an ever-widening wedge. Instead of streams arriving of the mountains, there are full-sized rivers. Tynedale (the name applies to the valley of the North Tyne) rises at Kielder, where passes reach across the Border to the head of Liddel Water. Eastwards, Redesdale runs up to Carter Bar, with a high crossing to the Teviot. The Rede joins the North Tyne just below Bellingham. The combined river flows through the Roman Wall at Chesters, where the Romans built a great four-arched bridge over it, to join the South Tyne at Hexham.

Eastwards again, the Coquet has its source on the slopes of Cheviot itself. Coquet bends away roughly eastward, and runs to the sea.

So in the west, Haltwhistle was in the front line for attacks out of Liddesdale in particular. In the east, Tynedale, Redesdale and Coquetdale were strips of green along the rivers, separated by high rolling moorland, scrub forest and bog – classic reiving country. It can appear as if Scotland provided the reivers, and the English – as settled inhabitants of the land – were on the receiving end of the raids. In the West March and along the Roman Wall that was roughly the situation. But the men of Tynedale, Redesdale and Coquet – the Forsters, Fenwicks and Charltons – were raiders as fierce and effective as any Armstrong, Elliot, Kerr or Scott.

Brampton showed little sign of the raids and skirmishes of the English West March. This is only mysterious until you realise that Brampton was built after it was all over. Haltwhistle does show its harsh history if you look closely enough (the oval blue marker plates can be a help). First of all, there's the way the townhouse gardens at the east end of the village rise with a steepness inconvenient for anyone trying to grow roses. Yes, this is a Norman motte, and a big one, rising in several steps. Out in the countryside the more lowly bastle houses, simple fortified dwellings, are mostly fallen to low walls. In Haltwhistle, they still stand high, but hidden behind bright paintwork and shop signs. One of them is now a fish-and-chip shop. And embedded in the right-hand half of the Centre of Britain Hotel, coloured up in sunshine yellow, stands a small pele tower.

The song 'The Death of Featherstonhaugh' recounts a moment around 1570 in the feud between Featherstones from just south of Haltwhistle and the Ridleys, from the foot of Allendale. It was still being sung at drunken parties on Alston Moor in the 1750s. The verse is so coarse that Sir Walter seems to have left it intact, apart from replacing with a dash whatever it was the Bailey did in the cooking pot (I've made the obvious one-word replacement). These last two verses describe the clearup after the slaughter.

> Hoot, hoot, the auld man's slain outright!
> Lay him now wi' his face down: – he's a sorrowful sight.
> Janet, thou donot,
> I'll lay my best bonnet
> Thou gets a new gude-man afore it be night.
> *I canno' tell a', I canno' tell a',*
> *And mony a mair that the deil may knaw.*
>
> Hoo away, lads, hoo away,
> We's a be hangid if we stay.
> Tak' up the dead man, and lay him ahent the bigging;
> Here's the Bailey o' Haltwhistle,
> Wi' his great bull's pizzle,
> That supp'd up the broo', And syne pissed in the piggin'.
> *I canno' tell a', I canno' tell a',*
> *And mony a mair that the deil may knaw.*
> [donot = silly slut (because she's weeping for her husband when it's so easy to find a new one); ahent = behind; bigging = building; piggin' = iron pot with two handles like ears]

In 1601, the Mangerton Armstrongs mounted a run-of-the-mill raid against Haltwhistle. Robert Cary, the new, young Warden of the Middle March, went by the book, and demanded satisfaction of King James VI. James replied that the Armstrongs of the Debateable Land were no subjects of his, and Robert Cary was to deal with them as he thought fit. So Cary launched a punitive warden raid against Liddesdale, with Sim Armstrong of the Cat-hill (misprint for Sim of Calfhill) being killed by a Ridley from Haltwhistle.

The Armstrongs counter-raided, and tried to burn down Haltwhistle, 'running up and down the street with lights in their hands'. Ten houses were destroyed (but at least five survived, to proudly display their oval plaques around the market place today).

In that raid, another Armstrong was killed by another Ridley, putting the Ridleys two up in the feud. The annoyed Armstrongs promised that over the coming autumn they would lay waste the entire Border. Cary believed them: old Sim Armstrong of Whitram had six tough sons and 200 riders at his command. Cary had just forty riders. The thing to do was to sit tight, while applying to Queen Elizabeth for reinforcements.

Phooey to that, said Cary. He would go up into Bewcastle Waste with his forty riders, and 'did not doubt, before the summer ended, to do something that should abate the pride of these outlawes'. Encouraged by Cary's example 'divers young gentlemen offered to go with mee, some with three, some with four horses'. In the end Cary took 200 good men and horse up to Bewcastle, where they built a temporary fort.

The Armstrongs, in their usual way, decamped from the Debateable Land back into Tarras Moss, the patch of moorland, bog and scrubby forest that fills the gap between Ewes Water and Liddesdale. They sent word to Cary that he was like the puff of hot air when the knife pierces the haggis; he'd cool down soon enough when he felt the Bewcastle rains. They sent more than rude messages, they sent the haggis itself – or at least, some prime English beef – in case Cary happened to be hungry. The cattle had been raided from Cary's own herds.

Meanwhile Cary was scouting the country. Finally he knew the ground well enough to send 150 of his force, guided by a 'muffled man' (a Scot with his face masked), 30 miles around to set ambush in the three passes leading north out of Tarras behind the Armstrongs. And in the first dawn light, he sent 300 horse and 1,000 on foot, deliberately routing them to be seen by the Armstrong scouts on the hilltops. The Armstrongs, as anticipated, retreated into the ambushes. Cary retrieved all the stolen livestock, and his captives included the two eldest sons of Sim of Whitram.

The battle won, it was time not for hangings but for hard negotiation. The Armstrongs agreed to quit claim to all deadly feud, to free all prisoners, and to pay compensation for earlier cattle raids. Fourteen of them gave promise as pledges, to deliver themselves prisoner to Cary if the terms should not be met. 'Thus God blessed me in bringing this great trouble to so quiet an end; we brake up our fort, and every man retired to his own house.'

LEFT ABOVE Haltwhistle's Lucky Palace and the Centre of Britain Gallery Launderette are two defensible bastles. Large boulders forming the wall bases of both buildings can be seen in the alleyway between.

LEFT The nearby hotel incorporates a pele tower to the right of the entrance. There are various ways to find the 'Centre' of the British Isles. Cutting it out of cardboard and balancing it on a pin gives Whitendale Hanging Stones in the Forest of Bowland. (Farmer Geoff Walker, who owns that precise patch of peat, told the BBC in 2002 he could not imagine it becoming a tourist attraction.) Haltwhistle stands at the midpoint of a north-south line between the northernmost Orkney Island (North Ronaldsay) and the south coast at Portland Bill. It also stands midway on an east-west line along Hadrian's Wall. So Haltwhistle is the centre of Britain – provided you work it out that way, and provided you also ignore Shetland.

THE ROMAN WALL

The Romans don't have much to do with this particular story. Hadrian may have invented the Scottish Border, but by the third century AD, the Tyne was a civilised county. Old soldiers from all over the Empire were encouraged to settle down locally and accustom the locals to Roman comforts, such as raising your crops and paying your taxes without having anyone come and burn down your house and kill you. The fort at Housesteads even had toilets with running water.

But in the old south gateway, Roman stones were recycled ten centuries later into a bastle house, low to the ground and thick-walled in the hope of keeping out raiders for at least the dark of a single night. It was a refuge for some English Armstrongs, and looked across a landscape that was farmland as early as the Iron Age, but in the Middle Ages (as now) more pastureland than crops. Behind the bastle the ground rises over the hummocks of the Roman fort, and there's no view northwards, from where the raiders arrived, until you reach the fort's upper edge.

A mile east of Housesteads, the civilised stonework of Rome marches down into Busy Gap. Across it at right angles runs the invisible trace of the reiver's road to the South Tyne. To insult someone in medieval Hexham, you referred to them as a 'Busy Gap Rogue'. And until 1771 a Newcastle bylaw stipulated that no apprentices should be taken from reiving Redesdale or Tynedale, they 'proceeding from such leude and wicked progenitors'.

LEFT Milecastle 37, west of Housesteads on Hadrian's Wall. There isn't always such an obvious contrast between the pastureland south of the Wall and the rougher moorland on the northern, Scottish side.

BELOW The dolerite layer of the Whin Sill rises gently to the north to break off in the north-facing scarp at Crag Lough. Hadrian's Wall runs along the top of this natural defence.

Tynedale

Two miles upstream from Hexham is the junction of the two Tynes. The South Tyne arrives at Hexham from the west, its upper river flowing down to Haltwhistle off the Pennines from its source high on Cross Fell. But 'Tynedale' means the North Tyne, and the North Tyne arrives out of quite another country. Follow it up beyond the Roman Wall, and you're in the Border moorlands that were the reiver strongholds.

The Robsons, Charltons, Dodds and Milburns of the North Tyne were, for general nastiness, in every way the equals of the Elliots and Kerrs across the Border. At Hesleyside Hall, just upstream from Bellingham, the dome would be lifted off the silver salver to show no steaming joint of beef but a single spur upon the dish. This was a hint from the Charlton lady that the menfolk should be off over the hill for some more supplies. Across the Border, traditions were different. The Scott lady would serve up for dinner not a single spur, but the pair.

The inhabitants and their attitudes may be the same but the dale is rather different. Annandale and Eskdale, Yarrow and Ettrick are carved out of the tough, ancient greywackes of the Southern Uplands. Tynedale is equally tough in human terms, but its rocks are softer. The younger Carboniferous rocks of the Northumberland Basin are gritstones and coal interbedded with limestone. Nor is this the glamorous mountain limestone of Yorkshire, but browner, sandier stuff. Its beds form wide grassy moorlands with the occasional mean little crag.

Below the moors, Tynedale is wide and open. A windy B-road runs up it with glimpses of the river, farms and small woods. In 2011 the local council closed Wark Bridge for four months, apparently not supposing anybody would mind that much. Shrugging off the National Grid, Wark village in 2003 installed solar-powered street lighting.

Six miles up valley, you reach the main town of Tynedale, Bellingham. It's far enough from supermarkets to have proper shops of its own. Its small church, like many along the Border, is dedicated to St Cuthbert. With its stone slab roof, it's more Scots than English in style. It has clearly been built as a strong defence not just against Satan and his wiles but also against the neighbours. Indeed, its tactical role may have supplanted its theological one. In 1524, Henry VIII's Cardinal Wolsey closed down all the Tynedale churches on the grounds that the priests were evil and irregular.

In 1314, just weeks after Bannockburn, Robert the Bruce made a kingly progress down Tynedale. Working on a novel about the Bruce, Nigel Tranter was puzzled at the new king's priorities and wondered whether he was asserting some ancient Scots claim over the valley. With some excitement, he turned up one ancient legal document (the Northumberland Assize Rolls of 1278) that rejected a particular case as outside its jurisdiction – because the trespass took place in 'Tynedale, in the Kingdom of Scotland'.

The South Tyne at Bardon Mill.

North Tyne not in England? Administratively, Tynedale was a Liberty, allowed some self-government on the basis that the actual Government didn't have much chance. Scots lords did hold possessions here. Tarset Castle was home to the Red Comyn, the man stabbed by Robert the Bruce in Dumfries church. This personal connection rather than any ancient claim may be why the new King Robert wished to show his power here. Tarset Castle is no more: the Charltons from 2 miles down the Tyne drove March Warden Sir Ralph Fenwick out of the place and set fire to it.

Between Carlisle and Berwick, Bellingham is the only true Border town on the English side. But compared with Galashiels, Hawick, Kelso on the Scottish side, Bellingham is a mere village. The lack of English Border towns vigorous through the reiving centuries may explain why the Border Country today is felt to be mainly on the Scottish side. Depopulated during two terrible centuries, one feels that these northern bounds of Northumbria have never fully come back to life. East across to the Coquet is the militarised zone of the Otterburn firing ranges. Meanwhile, all the country from Bewcastle Waste to the base of the Cheviots is under woodpulp trees – the largest plantation in Europe.

Over 250 square miles, where men on sure-footed ponies passed through the hill gaps and bogs, now rise narrow tree trunks in the gloom of the spruce needles. The ground is red-brown, plough furrowed and bare. A bright toadstool breaks the shadows, or a scum of green swamp. Dead branches interlace to make any human progress impossible. The forest roads, stony and bare, wind in circles with a strip of grey sky overhead. The Government refers to this stuff as 'forest' – creative image-manipulation which rebounded when it attempted to sell it all off in 2011 and was thwarted by an outraged public who imagined leafy glades, and squirrels, rather than this ugly feedstock of the woodpulp industry.

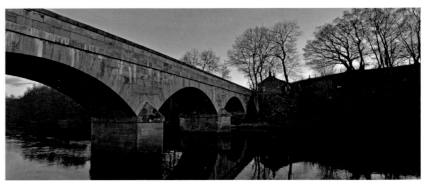

ABOVE Hareshaw Linn north of Bellingham.

RIGHT ABOVE Evening on the North Tyne at the Riding farm. The dismantled Northern Counties Railway, across the foot of the picture, carried limestone and coal from the head of Tynedale.

RIGHT MIDDLE Bellingham Bridge over the North Tyne, and the former toll cottage at its southern end.

RIGHT BELOW Kielder Water: Europe's biggest bit of submerged scenery, surrounded by woodpulp plantations.

But Kielder was bleak and abandoned even before the Forestry Commission came along. Around 1760 the 2nd Duke of Northumberland built the so-called Kielder Castle as his new shooting lodge. He found that 'his people in Keeldar were all quite wild. . . . The women had no other dress than a bedgown and petticoat. The men were savage and could hardly be brought to rise from the heath, either from sullenness or fear. They sung a wild tune, the burden of which was 'Ourina, Ourina, Ourina'. The females sung, the men danced round and at a certain part of the tune they drew their dirks which they always wore.' This is how his son described them to Walter Scott.

Kielder Stane

The North Tyne has its source in a swamp called the Deadwater. From Deadwater's other edge, peat seeps westwards to trickle into the very top of Liddesdale in Scotland. Above rises Deadwater Fell, a westward extremity of the Cheviots. It's decorated on top with an RAF radar station, an architect-designed bike shelter that claims views of both the North and the Irish seas, and mountain bike trail signs with phone numbers for the nearest hospital.

North of Peel Fell, a map of 1801 shows this stretch as 'Threap Land', still of unresolved nationality. Today, the Border line comes down off the watershed for 2 miles to wander along the upper slopes of Tynedale. That wiggle is to take it through the Kielder Stone. However disputable the general line, the Stone was known as a boundary marker in Walter Scott's time. And earlier than that, given that it was a meeting point on days of truce, for in nervous times a March Warden would be fussy about meeting his opposite exactly on the Border. (In 1598, Cary insisted on the initial handshake with Robert Kerr midstream in the Tweed!)

According to Mack's *The Border Line*, the Border passes through the centre of the Kielder Stone. It's a tor of the Fell Sandstone, eroded out from bedrock. At least once, adventurous local lads and lasses have got stranded on top of it.

> Green vervain round its base did creep,
> A powerful seed that bore;
> And oft, of yore its channels deep
> Were stained with human gore.
> And still, when blood-drops, clotted thin,
> Hang the grey moss upon,
> The spirit murmurs from within,
> And shakes the rocking-stone.

'The Cout [colt = lad] of Keeldar', from Scott's *Minstrelsy*, but this particular ancient ballad was worked over by John Leyden, Scott's linguist savant pal of Denholm. The channels in the stone have been worn by rainwater.

ABOVE The Kielder Stane was a meeting point between the two nations, and the Border line makes a detour from the ridgeline to pass through its centre. The island of grass among the heather may reflect the fertilizing effect of Borderers' ponies standing around on days of truce. The tiny peat path which passes along the Border line here is the result of the annual Kielder Borderer hill race. Without it, every step would be a struggle, whether for man or horse.

BELOW Peat stream above the Kielder Stone. The Border passes through this orange pool.

Redesdale

Opinions differ on the moral stature of Northumberland's three dales: Tynedale, Redesdale and Coquet. Nigel Tranter flatly states that the Charltons of Tarras and Tarset were the very worst of the English reivers. But a few pages later, it's the good folk of Rothbury on the Coquet who are 'amongst the wildest and most uncivilised in the country. For fighting, gaming and drinking they had a worse reputation than the inhabitants of Tynedale and Redesdale.'

By comparison, the Robson clan was courteous and sweet-tempered. 'I was born in Redesdale in Northomberlande, and come of a wight riding sirname, call'd the Robsons; gude honeste men, and true, savyng a little shiftynge for theyr living; God help them, silly pure men,' says a character from an untraceable 'London play of 1654' quoted by Walter Scott.

In fact the Robsons managed to be at feud with not one but both of the most formidable Scottish families, the Armstrongs and the Elliots. They were on reasonably good terms with the Scotts. On the other hand, they were at feud with at least one English family, the Grahams. The Robsons appear as a rather a lowly sort of reivers, coming home from the Debateable Land not with cattle but with a flock of Graham sheep. The sheep turned out to be scabby, and infected the Robson's own flock. Whereupon the affronted Robsons raided the Grahams again and hanged seven of them: 'The neist thyme gentlemen cam to take their schepe they war no to be scabbit.'

TOP Tower Hotel at Otterburn is another incorporating a pele tower, though the pastiche porch does its best to conceal the authenticity of what lies above.

ABOVE LEFT This far more genuine-looking fortress at Ridsdale village is not a castle at all, but the engine house of the Ridsdale Iron Works. It was built in 1836 and abandoned thirty years later. It housed two beam engines which pumped the air supply for three blast furnaces. Despite not being a Border keep, it was dismantled by the Armstrongs, in this case the industrialist W.G. Armstrong, descendant of Johnie Armstrong of Gilnockie, and builder of Cragside House in Coquetdale.

ABOVE RIGHT Former shop at Ridsdale, the bleak little village of former ironworkers' cottages astride the A68.

The Battle of Otterburn

In the summer of 1388, England's Richard II was occupied with the Peasants' Revolt. So the Border warlord James, 2nd Earl of Douglas, launched a looting foray into Northumberland. Returning up Redesdale, his 300 knights and 2,000 foot soldiers camped in an old hill fort west of Otterburn. Or he may have had 1,500 knights and 20,000 foot – depending on which chronicler you go along with.

Harry Hotspur, twenty-three-year-old son of the Earl of Northumberland, marched through the night to catch the Scots. He decided on a surprise attack, without waiting for the Prince Bishop of Durham and the rest of his column. This had the disadvantage that his archers would be useless in the dark.

By bad luck, Hotspur's attack hit the baggage train rather than the main force. Parts of both armies then got lost among the peat bogs, before the battle settled down to knife-fights in the dark. In his hurry, Douglas hadn't got around to doing up his armour, and was stabbed from behind – some say by his own armour bearer, discharging a personal grudge. His lieutenants kept quiet about his death and fought on with his warcry: 'A Douglas!' Hotspur was overwhelmed by enemies and captured, later to be ransomed.

At dawn the remnants of the two armies separated, and the surviving Scots limped homewards. The English casualties were 1,900 killed, 1,000 wounded, and 1,000 captured, against Scots loss of 100 dead and 200 missing – according to the Scots chronicler. According to the English ballad, 44,000 Scots were killed, wounded or captured, with just 18 getting away; while of the English force of 9,000, fully 500 survived.

Otterburn, then, was slightly more than a family outing to acquire some cattle – and took place a half a century before the Border broke down into lawlessness. But it was not a full international incident. Rather, it was a conflict between two regional warlords. The reason it's remembered 700 years later is not political but poetical, celebrated in three separate Border ballads. Between them they attach every possible romantic episode to the battle, including a prophetic dream by the Douglas, and a personal combat between the two principals.

> But I hae dream'd a dreary dream,
> Beyond the Isle of Skye;
> I saw a dead man win a fight,
> And I think that man was I.

When Percy wi' the Douglas met,
I wat he was fu' fain!
They swakked their swords, till sair they swat,
And the blood ran down like rain.

Dying, Douglas urges his captains to carry on the battle:

My wound is deep; I fain would sleep;
Take thou the vanguard of the three,
And hide me by the braken bush,
That grows on yonder lilye lee.

The moon was clear, the day drew near,
The spears in flinders flew,
But mony a gallant Englishman,
Ere day the Scotsmen slew.

Percy, already tired, is disarmed by Montgomery, then forced to sur-
render to a shrub . . .

Thou shall not yield to lord nor loun,
Nor yet shalt thou yield to me;
But yield thee to the braken bush,
That grows upon yon Lilye lee!

This deed was done at Otterbourne,
About the breaking of the day;
Earl Douglas was buried at the braken bush
And the Percy led captive away.
'The Battle of Otterbourne' as collected by Walter Scott

Carter Bar, looking north into Scotland. At the head of Redesdale the A68
rises to 418m (1,370 feet) in a grinding of lorry gearboxes, to pass between
sightseeing laybys and the flags of the two nations. This is the only road
crossing of the Border in the 41 miles of hill ridge between Deadwater and the
Bowmont Water at Kirk Yetholm. Long before it was a layby it was a place of
Border truce, and the breakdown of the truce-day arrangements here in 1575
led to the last international battle between England and Scotland.

Elsdon

If Internet ratings pages had been invented 300 years ago, the village of Elsdon, in lower Redesdale, would have a zero star rating. Extracts from the 'comments forum' include:

Modern Elsdon is a very small village consisting of a tower which the inhabitants call a castle, an inn for refreshment of the Scotch travellers, five little farmhouses and a few wretched cottages, inhabited by poor people who receive the parish allowance and superannuated shepherds.

Revd Charles Dodgson, *Rector of Elsdon*, 1760s

Contains little but large neglected heaths and extensive morasses.

MacKenzie's *History of Northumberland*, 1811

The whole parish is a wild dreary waste, its heather-covered sides without one single feature to relieve the monotony.

Bulmer's *Directory of Northumberland*, 1886

Hae ye ivver been at Elsdon ?
The world's unfinished neuk
It stands amang the hungry hills,
An' wears a frozen leuk.
The Elsdon folk like diein' stegs
At ivvery stranger stare;
An' hather broth an' curlew eggs,
Ye'll get for supper there.

George Chatt, poet, 1866

Elsdon is one of those places like Bewcastle with such a weight of history that it's missed out on the present century or two. Until 1157 it was the capital of Redesdale, and boasted a major Norman castle. The earthwork still dominates the village. Or it would, if it weren't for the even more dominating Vicar's Pele, the fifteenth-century fortified tower that forms one end of the minister's house.

Elsdon's church is as old as the pele tower, though it's been refurbished in every subsequent century. It's another dedicated to St Cuthbert: Cuthbert's bones spent the night here on their wanderings after the Viking attacks on Lindisfarne. Inside it, pillars near the door show the grooves where the stone was used for sharpening swords. In its north wall were 100 skeletons, all apparently of young men, taken to be the English casualties of the Battle of Otterburn.

The village was a junction of drove roads, and until bypassed by the route now called the A696 it had three inns – one of them is still there, though it doesn't serve heather broth. Above the village is an oaken gibbet, from which dangled a murderer called William Winter. The continuing criminal tendencies of Redesdale mean that the gibbet itself has been stolen. What now stands is a replacement, from which dangles a fibreglass interpretation of the head from the original corpse.

BELOW LEFT Elsdon from the south-west, with its Norman motte, pele tower and ancient church.

BELOW Backs of cottages, Elsdon.

TOP On the Simonside Hills, looking north up Coquetdale.

MIDDLE Overwintering Bewick's swans on a flooded gravel pit, now a nature reserve, near Rothbury.

ABOVE Cup and ring marks on Lodenshaw Hill above Rothbury. In the distance, and out of focus, are the Cheviot Hills.

RIGHT The head of Coquetdale cuts into the tough volcanic rocks of the Cheviot range. Here, for the first time, one of the English valleys resembles the Scottish reiving glens, such as Eskdale, Yarrow and Ettrick.

7 SCOTTISH EAST MARCH: THE MERSE

The Tweed Bridge at Coldstream. The engineer was John Smeaton the lighthouse builder. The arches are of different widths but all have the same radius of curvature. It was finished after six years' work in 1772, and crossed by Robert Burns 15 years later.

The Cheviot ridge marks the Border between the English and the Scottish Middle Marches. Over the 40 miles between Kershopehead and the Hanging Stone on the Cheviot, it only drops below 400m at a single point – the pass at Deadwater above Kielderhead. It is crossed by just two modern roads, the one at Deadwater and the high pass of Carter Bar. On the other hand, between the English East March and the Scottish one, the Border is marked by the Tweed; and the maximum altitude is just 15m.

Geography is destiny. From the point of view of a Border raider the wide plains east of the Cheviots, fertile land so rich in plump cows, were far less helpful than the high Cheviot ridge.

A band of Northumbrian Selbys, say, raiding into the fertile Merse, would be passing through inhabited lands, so they'd be seen on the way in. And on the way out with the stolen cows, it was those locals, rather than the raiders, who were the clever ones when it came to setting an ambush. Then there was the risk of getting trapped against the fords of the Tweed.

And even for Northumbrians, but worse for any tribe of Scottish Trotters raiding the other way, the garrison of Berwick was ideally placed to cut off their retreat. The English Middle March was administered from Alnwick, 20 miles back from the Border and much further than that from the hotspots north of Haltwhistle. The East March capital was at Berwick itself, with the Deputy Warden based at Norham Castle, which on a winter's morning can literally cast its shadow into Scotland.

This doesn't mean that the East Marches were an especially safe place to raise livestock or a family. In 1517, the Scottish East March Warden was chased down the main street of Duns by the Homes, his supposed subordinates from the Scottish side. His head was hacked off and hung up on the market cross.

The two East Marches don't just face each other across the Tweed. The English East March meets the Scottish Middle one, from Cheviot top down to Bowmont Water; and this boundary is a mountain one. It was across this line that Robert Cary confronted Sir Robert Kerr of Cessford, as recounted on pages 104–5. And each of the East Marches was continually raided out of the Middle Marches, the one on its own side almost equally with the enemy one.

The East Marches, then, were lawless and miserable – but very slightly less lawless and miserable than the two Middle Marches. Where the Middle Marches broke down into small family tribes, in the East Marches the political unit was a single local warlord, as in the feudal arrangement of Norman times.

In Northumberland, that overlord was the Percy family, the Dukes of Northumberland, who gave such trouble to Henry IV at the start of the Wars of the Roses (and in Shakespeare's two plays on that king).

In Scotland, Berwickshire was at first under the Black Douglas. Scottish national politics led to the downfall of Douglas, and during the reiving years the Scottish East March was under the Lords Hume, based first at Hume Castle south of Greenlaw and then, as the times became civilised, at the Hirsel outside Coldstream.

In 1963, the 14th Earl of Home (pronounced Hume) disclaimed his peerage to become the Prime Minister as Sir Alec Douglas-Home. In 1964, students from Aberdeen University – evidently not students of Border history – attempted to kidnap him. Sir Alec plied them with beer and talked them out of it. A year later his government was defeated in a general election by Labour under Harold Wilson.

Duns, Coldstream and the Coast

In the absence of Berwick itself (which is currently in England), Duns is the capital of Berwickshire. In 1377, the Earl of Northumberland crossed the border on a Warden Rode, a legitimate reprisal raid for some affront committed against Englishmen. He camped outside Duns, ready to burn down the town in the morning. But in the night the Duns burghers crept out with rattles made of deerskin and pebbles, used for chasing deer off crops. They scared the English horses through the camp, and the horses scared the English. Armed with scythes and hammers, the townsfolk chased them as far as a stream now named as the Bloody Burn. 'Duns dings a'' is now the town's motto, yelled with enthusiasm at its annual Riding of the Bounds.

The English did successfully burn down Duns during the Rough Wooing of 1545. Its former site, Brunton (burnt town) is marked by a cairn west of Duns Law.

Robert Burns was not a Borderer. However, in May 1768 he sold the rights of an edition of his poems and, with cash in his pocket, bought a mare for £4. He named her Jenny Geddes after the woman who threw her stool at the Bishop of St Andrews when he tried to use the English prayer book in Edinburgh. And on Jenny Geddes Burns took a three-week tour of the Borders. Duns was his first stop. During the Sunday service he chatted up his host's sister Rachel Ainslie, and when she couldn't find the preacher's text, he took her Bible and wrote a poem in it:

> Fair maid, you needna take the hint
> Nor idle texts pursue;
> 'Twas guilty sinners that he meant
> Not angels such as you!

On the Tuesday he was at Jedburgh, flirting with a Miss Lookup. On the Wednesday he was captivated by a Miss Rutherford. But that was all over by Thursday, when he met Miss Isabella Lindsay. He 'came within a point and a half of being damnably in love. . . . Took farewell of Jedburgh with some melancholy, disagreeable sensations. Jed, pure be thy crystal streams and hallowed thy sylvan banks! Sweet Isabella Lindsay, may peace dwell in thy bosom uninterrupted, except by the tumult throbbings of rapturous love!' Finding his single overnight not quite enough time for a seduction, he left Isabella a poem to remember him by, and presented her with his portrait engraving by Naismith, the frontispiece of the collected poems. The weekend was wet, so he toured Melrose and Dryburgh Abbeys.

From Duns, he travelled with Rachel (last Sunday's lassie if you recall) and her brother to Coldstream. Its bridge was just fifteen years old, and the party crossed it into England: 'Glorious River Tweed, clear, majestic. Fine Bridge,' he wrote in his diary, on what was his first time out of Scotland. Having arrived in England he fell to his knees, threw away his hat, and in celebration of his first ever return into Scotland, recited from his own verses: 'O Scotia! my dear, my native soil! O never, never Scotia's realm desert.'

Coldstream stands at the lowest ford of the Tweed, and along with Gretna is the only settlement of any size actually on the Border. The tollhouse at the Scottish end of the bridge was, like Gretna, the venue for runaway marriages. The Coldstream Guards, the oldest unit of the British Army, were actually raised in Berwick in 1650 as Monck's Regiment of Foot. They took their current name from their march from Coldstream to London over the first five weeks of 1660. The regiment quelled the disturbances at the end of the Commonwealth, and the newly restored King Charles II found the soldiers to be 'beautiful, disciplined and martial'. When another nasty riot broke out, the King decided that the Coldstreams would be the one unit of Cromwell's New Model Army that he wouldn't disband. Since then the regiment has won no fewer than thirteen Victoria Crosses.

LEFT Duns, with the Market Cross once decorated with the severed head of the Scottish East March Warden.

TOP The Union Bridge over the Tweed, with Paxton House above. It was invented and designed by Capt Sir Samuel Brown RN, costing one quarter the price of a stone bridge. It opened on 26 July 1882, and was then crossed by, in order: Captain Brown; twelve double-horse carts loaded with stones; two bands playing 'God Save the King'; and the Earl of Home. It is the oldest suspension bridge still carrying road traffic and sways excitingly whenever a car crosses. It is a Category A listed building in Scotland, a Grade 1 listed building in England, and a Scheduled Ancient Monument in both countries.

ABOVE The bridge is suspended from a chain of wrought iron bars connected with hinges. This is the same revolutionary technique as Telford's Menai Bridge, but the Union Bridge was finished first. In 1902 steel cables were added as a backup above the iron chains.

BLOEW Fishermen's hut on the Scottish bank of the Tweed, just above where the river enters the Berwick Bounds.

BOTTOM Eyemouth harbour.

RIGHT St Abbs sculpture commemorates those bereaved, not by Border raiders, but by the sea. A total of 189 fishermen died in the great storm of October 1881.

BELOW RIGHT St Abbs harbour. The harsh, rocky Berwickshire coast has the same atmosphere as the Border country it belongs to, but a different history. These villages look eastward across the North Sea, and have earned their keep by fishing, smuggling and even by wrecking.

ABOVE Fast Castle, 15 miles north of Berwick, a stronghold of the Homes.

LEFT Westwards into Scotland from Fast Castle. The distant modern building is in fact two: the blocky shape of Torness Nuclear Power Station, and the tall chimney of Dunbar Cement Works.

RIGHT Patriotic fence post at the eastern end of the Border.

Fast Castle

In English history, the Middle Ages are usually taken to end in 1482. That was when Henry Tudor defeated Richard Crouchback of York at Bosworth Field, so ending the Wars of the Roses. But if there'd been an all-seeing historian in the 1480s to say: 'Here we are emerging into the Early Modern era, thank goodness,' they might have said it regarding Scotland under James IV, rather than turbulent England.

The reign of James IV started in the Medieval manner. In 1488 two Border warlords, Archibald Douglas and Lord Home, kidnapped the teenage prince and used him as a mascot while defeating his father James III at Sauchieburn, near Stirling. But within a year, young James had taken to the field on his own behalf and defeated his rebel nobles. And as he reached manhood, he became a notable civilising king. He learnt Gaelic – the first and only Scottish monarch to do so. He occasionally wandered the kingdom in a scruffy old mac as the 'gaberlunzie man', to feel out the mood of the people. He founded Aberdeen University, set up a printing press, built magnificent warships and churches, and introduced the game of tennis. He wrote poetry and played the lute.

> Exercise justice with mercy and conscience,
> And let no small beast suffer skaith nor scorns
> Of greater beasts that be of more puissance.

> Make law alike to apes and unicorns,
> And let no bogle with his busteous horns
> The meek plough ox oppress, for all his pride,
> But in the yoke go peaceable him beside.
> [skaith = harm; bogle = wild ox; busteous = rough, fearsome]
>
> James's court poet William Dunbar,
> 'The Thistle and the Rose'

But Scotland could not become a post-Medieval power so long as England carried war over the Border. So it's just as well that Henry VII was willing to sign up in 1502 to a Treaty of Perpetual Peace: 'a true, sincere, whole and unbroken peace, friendship, league and amity . . . from this day forth in all times to come'. And in a lavish ceremony at Richmond Palace, Henry's teenage daughter Margaret was married to the Earl of Bothwell, standing in as proxy to King James. The following June she travelled north. Some bright spark decided that her first night in her new kingdom should be at Fast Castle.

'Imagination can scarce form a scene more striking, yet more appalling, than this rugged and ruinous stronghold, situated on an abrupt and inaccessible precipice, overhanging the raging ocean and tenanted of yore by men stormy and gloomy as the tempests they look down upon,' is how Walter Scott described it. As you approach down its steep grass path, the broken towers rise against the sea foam. It's reached across a neck of rock less than a metre wide.

Fast was no Royal property, but a stronghold of the Homes. Three years before, seven Northumbrian murderers had been imprisoned in its dungeons, forgotten about, and starved to death. Margaret was only fourteen years old, dark-haired, wide-faced; pretty in a Welsh, Charlotte Church sort of way. She had yet to meet her husband, and her followers were at a priory across the hill. In the dusk, she saw the candles in the high stone windows, and heard the waves crashing in the darkness 50 metres below.

Fitzroy MacLean gives Margaret 'the faults of the Tudors without their brains'. What she did have was the Tudor toughness, and she needed it when the Perpetual Peace broke down after just twelve years, and James died at the Battle of Flodden. That battle, and its aftermath, are why in Scotland the Middle Ages carry on for another two Jameses and Mary Queen of Scots. Lord Hume even made an attempt to kidnap Margaret and her children and take them back to Fast Castle. Margaret, in the event, would make a fair job of protecting her infant son, and Scotland, from the rival warlords and from England.

Exactly 100 years after Queen Margaret's journey north, Margaret's great-grandson travelled south to take the crown as King James I of England.

Nobody suggested he should spend the night at Fast Castle.

Flodden Field

I've heard them lilting at our yowe-milking,
Lasses a-lilting before dawn o' day:
But now they are moaning on ilka green loaning—
The Flowers of the Forest are a' wede away.
At buchts, in the morning, nae blythe lads are scorning;
The lasses are lonely and dowie and wae.
Nae daffin', nae gabbin', but sighing and sobbing,
Ilk ane lifts her leglen, and hies her away.
[yowe = ewe; ilka = every; loaning = hillside; wede = withered; buchts = sheep pens; dowie = sad; daffin' = dallying; leglen = milking stool]

'The Flowers of the Forest'

Weetwood Bridge across River Till, in the fertile Glendale east of Wooler. It's been widened, but is otherwise much as when the Earl of Surrey crossed it on his way to Flodden Field.

The Battle of Flodden Field

The tune of 'The Flowers of the Forest' is traditional, going back at least to 1625. The words are by Jean Elliot of Minto, near Hawick, daughter of the Lord Justice Clerk of Scotland. In 1745 she entertained Bonnie Prince Charlie while her father, a top civil servant of the Hanoverians, hid out on Minto crags. In 1756 her brother Gilbert wagered her a pair of Edinburgh's most stylish gloves that she could not, three centuries on, make people cry over Flodden Field. Another 250 years later, and the wistful tune, along with the image of the milkmaids picking up their stools and each walking down the hillside alone, still brings tears to eyes.

After Bruce's victory at Bannockburn, Scotland enjoyed 199 years of what was, by Scottish standards, peace and civilisation. All that ended in 1513. With the Wars of the Roses over, Henry VIII of England turned his attentions to France. Scotland's cultural and political links with France, the 'Auld Alliance', obliged James IV to invade England.

James was a uniquely popular king, and his army, 35,000 strong, combined an enthusiastic mix of Lowlanders, Highlanders and Borderers.

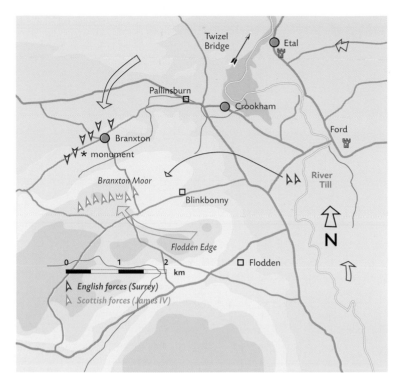

The Battle of Flodden was originally called Branxton Moor, which is where it took place. The battlefield monument was built in 1910 to commemorate 'the brave of both sides'. It stands where Surrey's army did, at the foot of the slope. The Scots battle line followed the hedge two thirds of the way up the slope.

Henry VIII was campaigning in France, and the Scots were opposed by the 70–year-old Earl of Surrey, a veteran of two battles of the Wars of the Roses (on the Yorkist, anti-Tudor, side). He had levied a second-best army of 26,000 men from Northern England, and picked up St Cuthbert's sacred banner from Durham, a proven battle-winner. Archers under Sir Edward Stanley were following on behind.

The Scots had a strong defensive position on the steeps of Flodden Edge. To reach them, Surrey would have to cross the small but deep River Till, which would mean his field guns staying behind on the wrong side.

The elderly general set about neutralising these Scots advantages. He marched northwards on the far side of the Till before crossing it at Twizel Bridge, 5 miles downstream, and approaching the Scots positions from the other side. James burnt his camp rubbish and used the smoke for cover as he turned his army around to occupy Branxton Hill, now facing north.

Surrey had manoeuvred the Scots on to a less favourable hill. He had arrived with dry bowstrings, and, more crucially, with his field guns. And he had cut the Scots off from Scotland – a psychological aid to his next operation, which was to get them down off their hill.

His cannon were of the modern kind, light enough for moving around in the field and capable of reloading in mere minutes. Most importantly, they were capable of being aimed. The Scots artillery consisted of heavy siege guns, including Mons Meg, which fired 20cm granite balls up to 2 miles, but had trouble hitting any target smaller than a large castle. The twenty-two English field guns, firing small lead balls, soon took out the Scots ones. Then they turned on the massed pikemen.

The Borderers on the Scots' left, under the Lords Home and Huntley, were the first to get fed up with being fired at. They charged down the hill, to defeat the English right wing somewhere near the present-day car park and monument. The English were rescued by their reserve under Lord Dacre, from the English West March. His Border horsemen then abandoned the battle to plunder the dead and haggle over ransoms with their new prisoners.

Encouraged by the Home victory, the Scots main force under the King came down to attack in the centre. Surrey had cunningly placed his force not at the slope foot but beyond a small bog, which broke the force of the Scots' charge. With that he had done all he could to equalise the battle. Now it was hand-to-hand fighting in the soggy ground of the valley floor: the 5-metre pike versus the 2-metre English billhook, a hedge-layer's weapon. With the pike formations broken up and bogged down, the English with their billhooks simply chopped the business ends off the long pikes and advanced on their owners.

At this point the delayed Sir Edward Stanley arrived from the south. Seeing the armies embattled in the plains, he took a hidden gully line to the moor top. Possibly he was surprised to find the Highlanders under Lennox and Argyll up there in reserve. But they were still more surprised to find Stanley suddenly outflanking them, and fled down the hill. Stanley now descended on to the embattled main force of the Scots.

Away on the western side of the hill, Huntley suggested to Home that they should help out the now surrounded King James. Home felt he'd done his bit. 'He does well that does for himself; we have foughten our vanguards and won the same: therefore let the rest do their parts as we.'

And Borderers from both sides, Scots Teviotdale and English Tynedale, started to loot the dead under Home's leadership.

By nightfall, 9,000 Scots and 4,000 English were killed. James lay dead with five billhook injuries in his body as well as an arrow. The only Scots leader to leave the battlefield alive was Home. Twelve earls and fifteen lords – the upper management layer of the feudal system – lay dead along with James's illegitimate son, the Archbishop of St Andrews. But enough had survived as prisoners that their ransom payments, aggregated together, sent the Scots economy into freefall.

The Border had always suffered, its abbeys and burghs sacked and burned, its crops destroyed, its small farmers left to starve. During the War of Independence the Scottish marches were ravaged again and again; after Bannockburn, Northumberland and Cumbria were laid waste. But it was Flodden that killed civilisation in the Borders like spilling a bucket. In 1964 American General Curtis LeMay threatened to bomb Vietnam back into the Stone Age. The aftermath of Flodden sent the late Medieval, feudal civilisation of the Border if not to the Stone Age, back into an Iron Age of small family tribes, warlords, misery and theft.

LEFT Branxton Church, originally Norman but extensively rebuilt. The bodies of King James and the noble casualties from both sides rested here after the battle.

LEFT BELOW The Sybil's Well on Flodden Hill, commemorates not the battle but Sir Walter Scott's fictional account of it in *Marmion*.

> Drink weary traveller drink and stay
> Rest by the well of Sybil Grey

The well misquotes Scott – it should read 'drink and pray, for the kind soul of Sybil Grey'. Scott himself authorized another misquotation, adopted for the signboard of Branxton's inn which was flourishing on Marmion tourism: 'Drink, weary pilgrim, drink and *pay*.'

BELOW River Till, a few miles downstream from Etal. Though running entirely in England, the Till, being a tributary of the Tweed, is a Scottish river for salmon purposes.

> Says Tweed to Till, 'What gaurs ye gang sae still?'
> Says Till to Tweed, 'Though ye rin with speed,
> And I rin slaw, Whaur ye droon ae man, I droon twa!'

On September 8 1513, the river was swollen with rain, and the available crossing places determined the English approach to the battle.

LEFT Hedgerow blackthorn and elder above the River Till.

ABOVE Etal Castle. This and nearby Ford Castle were captured by the Scots in 1514. To dally with Lady Heron at Ford Castle, King James for the first time took off the penitential chain that he wore under his clothing in expiation of the battlefield death of his father James III. Some say that Lady Heron (and perhaps her daughter also) seduced the Scottish King from pure patriotism, to delay him while Surrey gathered his men and sent to Durham for St Cuthbert's battle-winning banner.

RIGHT Etal's tearoom and shop. The village also boasts Northumberland's only thatched pub.

Wooler and Glendale

The little market town of Wooler stands at the corner of the Cheviots, a natural gatepost on the way through the Glendale gap into Scotland. A busy hub and centre of commercial and religious life – in the Iron Age, at any rate. Nobody knows what important function was served by the cup-and-ring marks carved into the Fell Sandstone of the moors to Wooler's east. Wooler's Iron Age settlement was converted into a Roman fort. The town received its market charter in 1199.

Confusingly, the Cheviot foothills have two separate Humbledon Hills – each with its Iron Age fort on top. The one north-east of Wooler has a peculiar distinction. Walter Scott wrote millions of words on Border affairs; but a still greater literary figure, with the same initials, gives the Border just a single scene. It's the opening one of Shakespeare's *Henry IV Part 1*, in which the battle of Homildon Hill (as the play calls it) is a crucial part of the back story.

Homildon Hill in Sept 1402 is a follow-on from the Battle of Otterburn already described. Henry IV was already dealing with a troublesome Welshman, Owen Glendower (in proper Welsh, Owain Glyndwr). It was a convenient moment for Sir Archibald Douglas, uncle of the Douglas slain at Otterburn, to lay waste northern England. Henry Percy the Duke of Northumberland along with his son Harry Hotspur blocked their return route into Scotland.

As King James was to do at Flodden a century later, Douglas deployed his forces on Homildon Hill's strategic slope. Hotspur and his dad lay along the Akeld–Wooler road below. The Northumbrian archers were sent on to Hare Hill to the west, protected from knights by the steep gap between.

The English arrows 'fell like a storm of rain'. Unable to attack the archers, some Scots knights abandoned their hill position in a suicidal attack on the main body of the Percys. When these all got killed, the remaining Scots turned and fled. Trapped against the Tweed, most of them were killed, captured or drowned.

The point, from Shakespeare's purposes, was to show Hotspur slaughtering Scots like a proper prince, while the King's own son Prince Harry gets drunk with Mistress Quickly and fat Falstaff. But after the battle, King Henry IV improperly demanded the Scots prisoners and their associated ransom money. This turned the Percys to revolt. The next battle would be between the Percys and the English King – cue the Battle of Shrewsbury and *Henry IV Part I* Act IV.

Whatever its Iron Age prosperity, Wooler suffered in the reiving times. The Bowes Survey of 1542 calls Wooler the outermost town of the kingdom: 'Nere therby ys the common entree and passage of the Scottes for invadynge this realme or makingg any spoyle in tyme of warre.' The hills offered refuge immediately to the west; at the same time, Wooler was at the start of the Till valley leading conveniently northwards to the Tweed's ford at Coldstream. Guarding that gap, 10 miles upstream from Berwick Bridge, stood Norham Castle.

Post office at Crookham on the River Till.

RIGHT Looking west across Glendale to the Cheviots. The foreground wood contains St Cuthbert's Cave.

BELOW St Cuthbert's Cave, a natural hollow in the yellow Fell Sandstone with shelter for a score of people. St Cuthbert's corpse stayed here during its years of wandering after the Viking raids against Lindisfarne.

Norham Castle

Day set on Norham's castled steep,
And Tweed's fair river, broad and deep,
And Cheviot's mountains lone:
The battled towers, the donjon keep,
The loophole grates, where captives weep,
The flanking walls that round it sweep,
In yellow lustre shone.
The warriors on the turrets high,
Moving athwart the evening sky,
Seem'd forms of giant height:
Their armour, as it caught the rays,
Flash'd back again the western blaze,
In lines of dazzling light.

Walter Scott, 'Marmion' Canto 1

In 1596, Queen Elizabeth appointed as Master of Norham a young man who had already proved himself in the West March, and who, by writing his memoirs thirty years later, was to give an intimate glimpse of the problems and pleasures of a Border official.

Robert Cary was born in 1560, son of the English East March Warden. Robert's grandmother was Anne Boleyn's sister Mary, played by Scarlett Johansson in the 2008 film *The Other Boleyn Girl*. If you believe that movie, and sixteenth-century rumour, Robert's grandfather would have been Henry VIII himself. His father, Lord Hunsdon, was appointed Lord Chamberlain, and so was the patron to Shakespeare and his actors – he may even have given some hints on Border affairs for the first scene of *Henry IV Part I*. Earlier in this book, outside Brampton, we've already seen Hunsdon helping to defeat a later Earl of Northumberland in the Rising of the North on behalf of Elizabeth I (his Boleyn cousin and possible Tudor half-sister).

Robert Cary was Hunsdon's eighth son, and he had to make his prospects for himself. Once he only defrayed his court expenses by a wager that he would walk to Berwick in twelve days for £2,000 (worth £200,000 today). As a teenager he was sent off to fight in Europe under Queen Elizabeth's favourite the Earl of Essex. In 1588 he sailed with the fleet against the Spanish Armada. The Queen also sent him on diplomatic missions to James VI, and at one point Cary assisted the Scots king by sending some English guns to help him recapture Lochmaben Castle.

Cary was thirty-one years old when his brother-in-law Lord Scrope offered him a job as a Deputy Marshal in the English West March. 'Passed my time in great content . . . for few days passed over my head but I was on horseback, either to prevent mischief, or to take malefactors.'

A few years later he took over the Captainship of Norham Castle from his father and became Deputy Warden of the East March. This brought him head-to-head with the Middle March Warden on the Scottish side, Sir Robert Kerr of Cessford: 'a brave,

TOP Village green at Norham, described (during the Scottish War of Independence) as the most dangerous place in England. Five hundred years later, Beatrix Potter called it 'a dirty little town where every tenth house is a public'.

ABOVE During the English Civil War, Parliamentarians billeted in the village practised musketry against the wall of Norham's Church of St Cuthbert – with not all the balls hitting the straw target.

From Norham Castle, an arrow can be fired across into Scotland – and has been, on many occasions.

active young man' as Cary calls him. The worst of the Border rogues at the time was Walter Scott, the Bold Buccleuch. Kerr of Cessford was only the second worst rogue.

Kerr received Cary's messenger with whisky and kind words. While the messenger was sleeping it off, Kerr took several horsemen into England, broke into the house of a minor enemy of his, and murdered him. Back home again, he sent Cary's man back with a reply that 'he was glad to have the happiness to be acquainted with me, and did not doubt that the country would be the better governed by our arrangements'. So why didn't they meet up somewhere quiet on the Tweed, next Thursday?

On the day agreed, having found out about the murdered Englishman, Cary discourteously didn't turn up. Now with open conflict between the two wardens, it was to be a long, hot summer on the East March. Cary decided to ignore the usual international arrangements. When he caught a Scots reiver with stolen cows, that reiver was hanged. Until one night, they came upon one Geordie Burn, a sidekick of Cessford's, driving home some English cows with his uncle. The uncle was shot, and after a brave struggle Geordie was wounded in the head and captured.

'Who is it that dares avow this night's work?' Geordie demanded proudly. When he heard it was the Norham garrison, he quietened down a bit.

As his neighbours pointed out, this put Cary in a strong position. 'I now had the ball at foot, and might bring Sir Robert Ker to what condition I pleased, for that this man's life was so near and dear unto him.' Burn was condemned, but Cary agreed to defer execution until the next day to allow Kerr to make his counter-offer.

That night, Cary dressed as an ordinary Borderer and went down to the cells with two of his soldiers to see Geordie. 'We hear that you're stout and valiant, and true to your friends; and we're really sorry our mean Mr Cary is

set on having you hanged.' And Geordie Burn made a reiver's confession: 'He had lived long enough to do so many villainies as he had done, and had lain with above 40 men's wives, what in England, what in Scotland; and that he had killed seven Englishmen with his own hands, cruelly murthering them; that he had spend his whole time in whoring, drinking, stealing, and taking deep revenge for slight offences. He seemed to be very penitent, and much desired a minister for the comfort of his soul.'

Cary sent him a minister; and then hanged him as the castle gates opened at the moment of daybreak. Kerr, arriving a couple of hours later to negotiate Burn's life, 'returned home full of grief and disdain'. At once he started raiding cattle out of the East March, hoping to provoke a hot trod which he would then ambush in the moorland hollows at the back of Wooler. When Cary didn't go for it, Kerr drove the stolen cows back into England: 'It was not goods he desired, but blood.'

Then in the following spring came an episode that could only have happened on the Border. At a day of truce at Norham it had been agreed that evil-doers from either side were to be delivered up by their respective wardens. When three months later the malefactors failed to appear, the two Scottish Wardens, Robert Kerr and the bold Buccleuch himself, delivered themselves up instead, as 'pledges' or hostages. And when Kerr was invited to chose who should hold him under arrest, he nominated . . . Robert Cary.

Cary, 'hearing so much goodness of him that he never broke his word', accepted Kerr's parole and removed the guards, while allowing him to receive visits from Scottish friends. A few days later Kerr asked to speak to him. The two Wardens had an almighty row, 'charging and recharging one another with wrong and injuries' – we may assume the name of Geordie Burn was mentioned here. And at the end of it, they 'continued very kind and good friends all the time that I stayed in that March'.

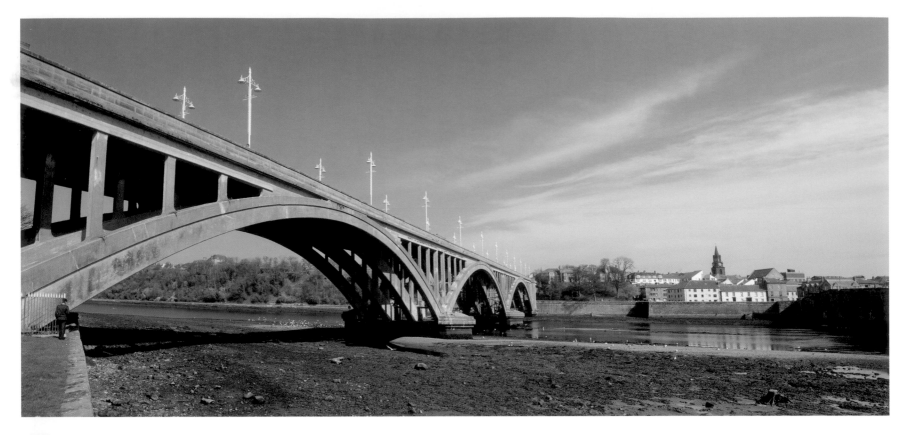

TOP The concrete Royal Tweed Bridge, built in the 1920s, and Berwick Old Bridge.

ABOVE The steel and concrete Berwick Bypass bridge of 1984.

RIGHT, ABOVE Berwick Royal Border Bridge on the east coast railway, built by Robert Stevenson in 1849. To its left, the old town wall descends to the river.

Berwick

While there are no towns of any size along the English side of the Border line, the towns at either end, Carlisle and Berwick, are both English.

Or are they? Berwick looks and feels Scottish, even though its walls point north to protect against the Scots. In 1147, after his capture at the Battle of Alnwick, William the Lion surrendered Berwick as part of his ransom. It then changed hands eleven times, before in 1482 Richard Duke of York took it for England. Before Flodden, King James offered to meet the Earl of Surrey in single combat for the stakes of the town of Berwick and the removal of the fish-garth (salmon trap) on the River Esk. If Surrey won, he would receive the proverbial King's ransom. The seventy-year-old Surrey said he was honoured by the invitation but had no authority to yield up Berwick, let alone remove the salmon trap.

Under a treaty between Edward VI and Mary Queen of Scots, Berwick became a free burgh, autonomous from England. According to a persistent folk-tale, at the start of the Crimean War in 1854, 'Victoria, Queen of Great Britain, Ireland, Berwick-upon-Tweed and all British Dominions' declared war on Russia. But at the Treaty of Paris that ended that war in 1856, Berwick was omitted. Accordingly, Berwick remained at war with Russia for over a century. At some point during the Cold War, the burgers of Berwick became nervous about atomic bombs delivered by intercontinental ballistic missiles. In 1966 the Mayor formerly signed peace with a grim-faced Communist official: 'Please tell the Russian people that they can sleep peacefully in their beds.'

The disappointing fact is that since the Wales and Berwick Act of 1746, all references to England legally include Berwick, and that Berwick is mentioned by name in neither the declaration of war nor the Treaty of Paris.

English law applies to the town, but Scots law to the River Tweed that flows through it. The Berwick dialect sounds Scots to most English listeners, but Northumbrian to Scots ones. When the English College of Heralds was slow to supply the town with a coat of arms, it applied instead to the Scottish Lord Lyon King of Arms, and its current badge is held as one of the four original Royal burghs of Scotland. Berwick was part of the (Scottish) Eastern Borders Development Organisation, and the headquarters of the King's Own Scottish Borderers. Berwick Rangers FC plays in the Scottish League, and so does the town's rugby team. The Scottish free bus pass for the elderly allows travel to both Berwick and Carlisle.

In the 1970s activist Wendy Wood moved the border boundary sign of the A1 to the middle of Berwick Bridge. Around 2008, the Borough Council of Berwick considered defecting into devolved Scotland, so as to benefit from free nursing care for the elderly. A planned BBC TV comedy drama *A Free Country* may air the possibility of an independent Berwick.

Given the number of times it's been fought over, all that survives of Medieval Berwick is its street plan and a short section of the town walls above the river. Those walls were built by Edward I of England in 1295. Between 1306 and 1310, Isobel Countess of Buchan was suspended from them in an open iron cage, Edward's punishment for her part in the coronation of Robert the Bruce. The town's Wallace Green commemorates William Wallace, one

Berwick is a lively market town, but these Victorian shops at the end of the old bridge have been left behind.

quarter of whom was displayed here after his execution for treason in 1305. Berwick's castle now lies underneath the railway station, though one original wall survives alongside the goods yard. In 1292 Edward I pronounced for John Balliol in the great hall, now the station platform.

During the reiving years, Berwick was England's strongest fortress, even stronger than Carlisle. It is, today, even less romantic than Carlisle's squat pile. Its town wall and fort, built to withstand cannon, have ramparts of sloping earth, and sunken areas walled in stone.

For romance, there's Berwick's river. The handsome railway bridge was built of brick arches with stone facing by Robert Stevenson in 1850. The main road bridge, the Royal Tweed Bridge, is four soaring concrete arches of 1928 – the northern one the widest of its time. But the finest of the three is to seaward, the Old Berwick Bridge. Entering England and his new kingdom, James VI suffered an attack of nerves crossing the rickety wooden bridge of 1376; he had to dismount and was carried across with his eyes shut. So he used his new English riches to build the stone one.

The End of the Border

> That all those in quhome thair can be expectit na houpe of amendement and ar thocht incorrigible may be removit furth of that cuntrey to some uther place, quhair the change of air will mak in thame an exchange of thair maneris.
>
> Instructions to the Border Commissioners, 1605

Even before building Berwick's new bridge, King James was sorting out the Border. The reiving times show how, if things get bad enough, civilisation's bucket kicks over, and law and society simply stops working. Even more interesting is the story at the other end. At a certain moment, civilisation's bucket can be set back upright again. So that, in the words of James V, 'the rysche bus kepis the kow', the rush bush keeps the cow – rather than the Fenwicks or Elliots getting it.

After 200 years, most Borderers must have been desperate for it all to end. Robert Kerr, handing himself in as pledge rather than raiding into England, must have been aware that England and Scotland would soon be under a single king. The general realisation was that times could, at last, be a-changing, and this may have helped Robert Cary in the English Marches. But equally Robert Cary himself, ruthless, honourable and honest, did much to make it happen.

Even as James was dithering on Berwick Bridge, the Border was breaking loose. The Grahams of Cumberland made the mistake of raiding deep into England, as far south as Penrith. This made the Grahams first target, and James subjected them to the seventeenth-century equivalent of racial cleansing. Their lands were confiscated, their houses were burned, and

BELOW Berwick's defences were rebuilt for the age of gunfire, and during the reign of Elizabeth I this was Britain's strongest fortress. Partly underground, its ramparts of stone and earth are many metres thick.

BOTTOM Berwick Old Bridge.

their riders were transported to the Low Countries to serve in the British garrisons. Grahams were imprisoned on the basis of their name alone. Finally, the remnant of the clan was transported to Northern Ireland – thus, ironically, setting up the following 400 years of conflict there.

Among the most enthusiastic and effective persecutors of the reivers were their own former warlords. The Bold Buccleuch, rescuer of Kinmont Willie, burned down towers and houses and hanged the reivers – except when, to save expensive rope, he drowned them in rivers. Cary's opponent Sir Robert Kerr of Cessford became Lord Roxburghe. And the Duke of Buccleuch is now Britain's largest private landowner, occupant of Bowhill house and Drumlanrig Castle.

LOOKING BACK
ALONG THE BORDER

Today we'd call it a failed state. During two centuries along the Border (as in certain Third World countries and in Mafia-governed parts of Russia today) there was no superior authority, and no laws. Why be nice to your neighbour when before he can return the favour, he's dead on the end of someone else's lance? What is the use in raising crops for the winter when they'll get burnt in some night raid the autumn before?

During that time, humanity stepped back from the nation state to an earlier time of small tribes ruled by a warlord. Local laws made it all work, up to a point. The system of blackmail payments (protection money, they called it in Chicago) made cattle raising possible, at least sometimes. Kidnapping for ransom was a normal commercial transaction: a kidnap victim of good reputation would be allowed home to raise his own release money.

The settlement of disputes by single combat should, at least, discourage disputes. Would you take the shears to your neighbour's Cupressus hedge? The blood feud works in a way: you'd hesitate before slaughtering any Kerr or Elliot, or even a mere Turnbull. And so, Njal's Saga recounts a linked sequence of blood feuds in tenth-century Iceland, set off by a man slapping his own wife. Mountain villages in Crete lie empty as a result of feuds of just 200 years ago.

Cattle thieving was a necessity. Murder was the system of sanctions that held society together. But for a man to break his word: that was serious. With a glove on the end of your lance, you could go after him and even the glens of your enemies would help you along. The American West, in the absence of controlling civilisation, adopted the same code of feud and personal honour. The

Hollywood Western, with its simple storylines and morality, is the direct equivalent of the Border Ballad.

During a million years as hunter-gatherer animals, we evolved in just such tribes and family groups. The Border lifestyle, with its special ethics, may correspond with our deepest social instincts.

I'm not a historian: I'm a hillwalker. To understand this country I slept on its hills, stood in its ruined towers, and walked through six April days from the Solway mudflats to Berwick on Tweed. A roe deer in a thicket leapt across the twin trench of the Scots Dyke, built along the line laid in 1552 by the French Ambassador. In Liddesdale they'd lost sheep to rustlers, and in the pre-Christmas period, seventeen hens had vanished from the College valley.

The Border ballads are deceivers. There was nothing romantic about the reivers, descending in the moonlight to kill and maim, and then set fire to the house. They left the Border lands empty, even to today. Reading in between the lines of the ballads, and in the fallen stones of the bastle farmhouses, is to relive in our own landscape the failed states of today. Sudden death and sheepstealing might even come back to the Borders if the mess we're making of our planet should, indeed, turn out to be civilisation-ending.

And yet the ballads do not lie at all. Set out at dusk on the pony that's almost an intimate body-part. Trek through moonlit hills with a dozen trusted brothers and uncles. Get the routefinding right among the peat bogs, and descend at dawn, with the slope in your favour and the sun shining over your shoulder, on a dozen despised Grahams or Forsters. All this is sport that makes mere hillwalking seem very tame indeed.

Further Reading

All three of my main references happen to be novelists rather than historians. Perhaps we can link this with Thomas Carlyle of the Scottish West March, who showed that history is meaningless without emotional involvement.

Walter Scott, *Minstrelsy of the Scottish Border* (1802): online via www.walterscott.lib.ed.ac.uk.

Scott was just in time to collect the Border ballads while the oral tradition was still alive. Happily, he only 'improved' them a little as they passed his pen. His historical notes on the ballads are lively and interesting, and if modern research has discredited some of them, so much the worse for modern research.

Nigel Tranter, *Portrait of the Border Country*, Robert Hale, 1972 (revised in 1987 as *The Illustrated Portrait of the Border Country*)

A snapshot (but with only a few pictures) of the Border country as seen in 1972. Tranter's history is coloured by his Scottish Nationalism, and why not? His easy-reading historical novels (including three on Robert the Bruce) are spoilt for me by a sub-Victorian prose style, but his Border book is straightforward and affectionate.

George MacDonald Fraser, *The Steel Bonnets: The Story of the Anglo-Scottish Border Reivers, Harvill*, 1971

MacDonald Fraser is best known for his string of lightweight historical novels featuring Flashman, the bully from *Tom Brown's Schooldays*. His 400-page study of the Border Reivers is serious and lively, informed by his own experience of irregular warfare in Burma in the Second World War. It is detailed and scholarly, but absorbingly readable, especially if you bear a Border surname.

Robert Cary, *Memoirs*, written about 1627, first published 1759, in print as *Memoirs of Robert Cary, Earl of Monmouth*, Bibliolife, 2011

Cary was a man of action, not a writer, so his account of his exciting years as warden or assistant warden on all three English Marches is disappointingly short.

Andrew and John Lang, *Highways and Byways in the Border*, Macmillan, 1913

Another snapshot of the Border, 60 years earlier than Nigel Tranter's. Andrew Lang wasn't a novelist, but he was a poet and collector of fairy tales. The book is enhanced by many pencil drawings by Hugh Thomson. The countryside is much the same as in 1911, except that the roads are wider and the ruins more ruinous, but most striking are the car-free towns.

James Logan Mack, *The Border Line*, Oliver & Boyd, 1926

A detailed study of the actual Border, with many photographs. Mack walked every step of the Border line in the 1920s.

Fitzroy MacLean, *A Concise History of Scotland*, Thames & Hudson, 1970

John Prebble, *The Lion in the North*, Martin Secker & Warburg, 1971

Monica Clough, *The Field of Thistles: Scotland's Past and Scotland's People*, Macdonald Publishers, 1983

Any of these is useful for anyone brought up in the English education system who missed out on the Scottish side of things. Prebble was a socialist, and his book has a spark of rage running through it. Clough's book is more social than political, and carries strong linocut illustrations by Willie Rodger.

Acknowledgements

Thanks to David Howard and Jane Dammers (Hexham) for hospitality on the English side; to Mounthooly bunkhouse (College Valley) on the Border; and to Fi Martynoga (Traquair) also for helping plant that wildwood on White Coomb. The National Trust and Scottish National Trust, English Heritage and Historic Scotland maintain not just the fabric but also the atmosphere at Carlisle Castle, Caerlaverock, Lochmaben Castle, Hermitage Castle, Hadrian's Wall, Melrose Abbey, various Redesdale bastles, Cragside, Smailholm Tower, Norham Castle and Berwick fort.

Thanks to Roly Smith for editing without the touch of the Jebbart Axe, and for letting through all three puns; and to Michael Brunström for his sympathetic page layouts and design. On the literary side, my debt to Scott and Macdonald Fraser will be obvious to anyone who has read their two works. Anyone who hasn't should do so if they want to understand the Border country.

INDEX